C000156172

Seven __ ,
Ignite Outrageous Prayer

Seven Ways to
Ignite Outrageous Prayer

by Carl Brettle
with Nigel James

CONTENTS

FOREWORD

As he stood up and strode purposefully across the room to the 'prayer chair', Thomas began to pray, 'Thank you Jesus. We pray that we have a good day today, and that you keep us safe...' I nodded in agreement – a good start to a prayer, I thought.

'And if we go out today...' he continued seriously, with his eyes wide-open and hands gripping the arms of the chair, '... and you help policemen to catch robbers.' I wondered if I'd hear those last few words right. Thomas, however, barely pausing for breath, pressed into the most recognizably theological part of his prayer. 'And when you died on the cross, you took on... you... we gave you life, if we did... if we were powerful like a *Power Ranger.*' Thomas was really on a roll by this stage. 'And when you died on the cross... and when you, when we... and we went to Duggie Dug Dug's, and we saw your nails through your hands. Amen.'

Thomas was four at the time, and he's one of my daughter Poppy's best friends. She (like Thomas) is a wonderfully confident, extrovert child, making the most of all opportunities to be (and remain) the centre of attention. Unlike Thomas, however, Poppy is profoundly deaf. It's a long story, for another time maybe, but Poppy's deafness has had profound effects on our family's lives... and on much of what we believed, not least of all about prayer.

When Thomas finished his *Power Ranger* prayer, in the middle of the children's cell group we'd been hosting, Poppy got up to pray too. Poppy's prayers are largely unintelligible, except for an occasional name thrown in. She is in the very early stages of learning to speak, which means that much of her communication is 'babbling', and much of her prayer is too. As I listened to the sounds coming from her mouth, I wondered... what does this *mean*? Is she actually *saying* anything? Is this *communication*? Does God even *understand* any of this?

But then I imagine Jesus purposefully striding towards *us*, with arms open wide. He brushes aside my culturally-rationalised questions just as he did his disciples' attempts to protect him from the crowds, and says, 'Let the little children come to me. . . Let them do it their way. I like *Power Rangers*, by the way! And you should hear what's going on in Poppy's heart when she babbles like that – it's like poetry! I love it! If you want to understand how to *really* talk with me, then you better listen to these children.' And I find myself humbled once again. (And I also wonder if my long-winded, meandering prayers sound like poetry too?)

A dictionary definition for the word 'outrageous' is 'being beyond all reason, extravagant or immoderate'. I love that. Prayer, conversation with God, is like that – it is *beyond all reason*. Conversation with God defies logic, it confounds formulas and yet it is incredibly simple. . . we start by simply learning to talk, learning to express what's in our hearts, honestly, and then learning to listen, carefully. And we become changed as we do.

How you approach this book is important – or any book on prayer for that matter. If you're searching for foolproof shortcuts to a divine hotline, let me save you the time and the effort – you won't find any. However, what you *will* find are pages full of Carl and Nigel's experience – stories from scripture and from their own lives, evidence that they're learning to talk with God, and listen to God, and that's what makes this book worth reading.

Phil Togwell
UK Base Leader 24-7 Prayer

INTRODUCTION

Paul understood it, and so did Peter. Moses got it eventually, whilst David, Abraham and Enoch found it at various times. Hannah and Samuel pursued it and Lydia exemplified it. All of these biblical characters knew the importance of outrageous prayer. So the concept of 'praying outrageously' is not a new idea or style of praying, although it is a revolutionary one. Outrageous prayer comes straight from the very core of Scripture and is all about having a heart attitude that opens our lives up to the possibility of God intervening in extreme, difficult, even impossible situations.

My good friend Carl Brettle testifies to it too. He knows what it means to pray outrageously. Let me illustrate with a story. In October 1999, as Carl was preparing for a trip to South Africa, he felt the Lord say to him, 'One million hours of prayer for Wales.' Carl was puzzled and perplexed at first, but returning from his travels with a new zeal in his heart for his homeland, he threw himself into the campaign and it took just five weeks to raise one million hours of prayer involving people from over 30 nations. Twelve months later the one million hours turned into ten million with over 50 countries participating. Carl speaks of this time as 'waking up in the morning knowing that this was a day when you were doing something you were born for.' Carl has been living and breathing outrageous prayer ever since.

As for me, well I'm still in the shallow end of prayer, and helping Carl write this book will be a plunge in the deep end. A couple of years ago I asked Carl to spend some time coaching me into a deeper understanding of prayer. After a few meetings I realized that the rest of our team at Ignite needed to listen to Carl too, and so he came and led one of the monthly prayer days. Seeing our team pair off to pray outrageous prayers for each other was a momentous experience, and one that many look back to as a landmark moment in their walk with Jesus. Following on from this, Carl spoke at the 'Flames of Fire' festival and on our Ignite

Leadership Academy. He never fails to excite and inspire people – especially young people – about the thrill of praying outrageously. I pray that as you read this book you will be one of these people.

An outrageous leader

The disciples would have learned so much about prayer from travelling with Jesus; they were present for many 'outrageous' occasions in the life of Jesus. Take his triumphal entry into Jerusalem for example. As he entered 'the whole city was shaken':

> *Unnerved, people were asking, 'What's going on here? Who is this?'*
>
> *The parade crowd answered, 'This is the prophet Jesus, the one from Nazareth in Galilee.' Jesus went straight to the Temple and threw out everyone who had set up shop, buying and selling. He kicked over the tables of loan sharks and the stalls of dove merchants. He quoted this text:*
>
> *'My house was designated a house of prayer;*
>
> *You have made it a hangout for thieves.'*
>
> *Now there was room for the blind and crippled to get in. They came to Jesus and he healed them.*
>
> *When the religious leaders saw the outrageous things he was doing, and heard all the children running and shouting through the Temple, 'Hosanna to David's Son!' they were up in arms and took him to task. 'Do you hear what these children are saying?'*
>
> *Jesus said, 'Yes, I hear them. And haven't you read in God's Word, "From the mouths of children and babies I'll furnish a place of praise"?'*
> *(Mt. 21:10–16, The Message)*

There could be no doubt about it: Jesus was in the middle of the situation. He had arrived.

Throwing out illegal shopkeepers, kicking over tables, destroying the stalls of dove merchants – pretty outrageous! Telling folk that they had turned a house of prayer into a hangout for thieves – very outrageous! Healing blind and crippled so that children would run around shouting praises to you – extremely outrageous! No two ways about it, when Jesus was around, things happen.

The Bible often uses the word 'outrageous' in a negative way to refer to people who have done things to offend God. In the passage above we see that the religious leaders labelled Jesus as 'outrageous'; they were angry and demanded an explanation for his behaviour. But we are saying that along with being 'amazing' and 'astonishing' Jesus was positively outrageous.

If you read the gospels you will see that when Jesus wasn't amazing the crowd he was astonishing them; and he was always outrageous in the true sense of the word: extravagant or unconventional, likely to shock people, exceeding the bounds of what is expected, unrestrained action. That's what Jesus was like, that's what his life was like, that's how he reacted to the needs of people who believed in him, and that's what we mean by outrageous.

Having seen Jesus live this out, it comes as no surprise that the disciples wanted to imitate Jesus in prayer: they were desperate for him to help them pray more effectively and outrageously.

One day Jesus was praying in a certain place. When he finished, one of his disciples said to him, 'Lord, teach us to pray, just as John taught his disciples.'

He said to them, 'When you pray, say:

"Father, hallowed be your name,
your kingdom come.
Give us each day our daily bread.

Forgive us our sins,
for we also forgive everyone who sins against us.
And lead us not into temptation."'

Then he said to them, 'Suppose one of you has a friend, and
he goes to him at midnight and says, "Friend, lend me three
loaves of bread, because a friend of mine on a journey has
come to me, and I have nothing to set before him."

'Then the one inside answers, "Don't bother me. The door is
already locked, and my children are with me in bed. I can't
get up and give you anything." I tell you, though he will not
get up and give him the bread because he is his friend, yet
because of the man's boldness he will get up and give him
as much as he needs.

'So I say to you: Ask and it will be given to you; seek and
you will find; knock and the door will be opened to you. For
everyone who asks receives; he who seeks finds; and to him
who knocks, the door will be opened.' (Lk. 11:1–10)

In Carl's words

Thanks for introducing me earlier Nigel. I just want to
share a few thoughts about the passage above.

It's incredible to consider that most of Jesus' teachings
encourage us to take a step beyond what is usual into a
place that is supernatural – a place where overcoming the
impossible is normal. In this passage Jesus is giving some
of the first clues on how to live a life of outrageous prayer,
helping us start a journey, and all this from the greatest
influence the world has ever known!

Imagine for a moment. You're a disciple. You believe that
Jesus is the Son of God and have the awesome privilege to
walk with him for a little while. So here you all are sitting
together for a prayer meeting, but no one wants to say
much, in case they do it wrong. They might say the wrong

thing or feel stupid asking God for something in the wrong way, so Jesus takes the lead and a lesson in prayer begins.

The disciples were gobsmacked that Jesus was able to pray with such confidence, boldness and belief, and wanted to also learn how to connect with God in a similar way. Let's not forget the context of the prayer. Up until this time they had seen Jesus 'in action': healing the sick, raising the dead, calming the storm, casting out demons and teaching them about what it was to fast. The subject of prayer was raised after this.

So why did Jesus need to teach in such a simple way when the disciples had already seen such awesome miracles? Let's face it, if we had seen Jesus raise Lazarus from the dead, for example, we'd be pretty convinced prayer works – wouldn't we? If you're like me, I used to go to meetings where God was moving and think, 'It's OK for the speaker to pray like that or for God to use the ministry team, but I'll never be able to do that. They have some special relationship with God that I will never have.' Perhaps the disciples were thinking the same thing about Jesus. So he goes out of his way to teach them how to pray. Let's break down what he says in the Lord's Prayer. Put simply, Jesus is saying that we are to:

- Recognize the awesomeness of God and his Kingdom
- Ask God to supply our basic needs
- Ask for forgiveness for the things we have done wrong and forgive people who have done wrong to us
- Ask God to help us from getting into more sin

    (You can cross-reference Luke's record of what Jesus said, by looking at the same incident in Matthew 6:9–13.)

Now that we've looked at the passage in modern English, let's condense this into four phrases that we can make our own.

- God you're awesome
- I can't survive without you
- Sorry I messed up, I forgive everyone who's hurt me – please bless them
- Help me to live a holy life

Do these four phrases describe how you want to live life as a Christian? Then you've just prayed a modern version of the simplest yet most profound teaching on prayer that there ever was – from Jesus himself.

The bottom line comes in the verses that follow. Jesus is telling the disciples that when you pray you should come to God like you are talking to your best friend; someone you know you can talk straight to, someone that you can be bold with until the answer comes.

Let's face it, if God is the creator of the universe, if he can be in all places at all times, then what's the point in trying to hide something from him or treat him like he's too important, or too distant to want to bother with us? Wouldn't it be great by the time you finish reading this book to be convinced that you have a one-to-one, deep personal, open and honest relationship with the one who created the planet you're sitting on, and the one that provides for your daily needs and knows intimately your hopes and desires, dreams and goals in life?

This friendship with God as Father has no limits – you can live a life that will take you places you never hoped you could reach; to meet people you never thought possible and to see God work miracles in situations hard to comprehend.

This journey of prayer is a simple, bold and honest lifetime conversation with God. It is one that you will continue in heaven, so let's get as much practice in as we can while we're here on earth.

Unlocking the seven keys

The purpose of the book is to provide an entry-level exploration of prayer that will provoke a deeper prayer life for you – whether you are a young person, young adult or youth leader. We will not be creating a manual for prayer or a cure-all system, but will present an outrageous perspective on prayer that isn't limited by experience, circumstances, or the human condition. If you are willing to say 'Lord, teach me to pray' then this book is for you!

Definition of prayer

Prayer is simply a two-way conversation with God.

Definition of outrageous prayer

Outrageous prayer is when you speak boldly and confidently to God, believing that God will get involved in the difficult or challenging areas of life that you have talked to him about.

We'll be giving you seven key ways to help you ignite an outrageous prayer life. Carl will be guiding you through each of them and using some easy-to-handle teaching based on biblical examples. Nigel will be adding some examples from his own life and from the ministry of Ignite, and he'll also be asking Carl to explain some of the jargon words used about prayer. We'll include a short prayer for you to use at the end of each chapter. So let's start the journey of outrageous prayer!

Heavenly Father, teach me to pray like Jesus prayed. Teach me to pray outrageously, in the name of Jesus. Amen.

Nigel James

1 HONESTY BEFORE GOD

> 'Prayer does not equip us for the greater work;
> prayer is the greater work.'
>
> Oswald Chambers, My Utmost for His Highest

Have you ever thought that it's impossible to hide from God; impossible to keep secrets that others around you will never know from the day you were born till the day that you die? Most of us have 'stuff' locked up in the store cupboards of our heart that we will never reveal or admit. Times we have stolen things; times we have lied and denied it; times when we've manipulated a situation and put the blame on someone else; times when we've been caught up in sexual desires looking at pornography – when all the time we portray ourselves as holier than the next person. There are even times when we have wished someone dead because they didn't consider 'our feelings'.

God knows your name

In the early part of Exodus Moses is on the run. A new Pharaoh (or ruler) has just taken power in Egypt, and becomes afraid: with so many Israelites they might turn against Egypt if ever there was a war. The answer? 'Let's put the Israelites into slavery working for us and let's kill all the first-born boys of the children of Israel by throwing them into the Nile.'

On hearing the news, Moses' mum hid her newborn son for the first three months of his life, but when she could hide him no longer she decided to make a basket and send Moses down the Nile, hoping someone would find him.

For so many baby boys the river Nile was a graveyard, but for Moses it was a means of escape. He was rescued by Pharaoh's daughter and grew up as an Egyptian in the court of the man who wanted him killed (See Ex. 2:1–10).

Even though Moses was essentially raised as a high flying Egyptian he still knew about his Israelite roots and as a man went to see for himself the way the Israelites were being treated by the Egyptians. Enraged Moses took his anger out on an Egyptian guard who was beating an Israelite. His response? He killed him and hid his body in the sand. He was sure he had got away with the murder, until the next day someone told him what he had done. Pharaoh heard about it and turned on Moses, tried to kill him and Moses fled Egypt.

The scene is set – God is slowly using the events that are happening to shape Moses' future, to bring him from a villain on the run to the deliverer of the whole nation. How does God do things like that? It's beyond me!

Moses eventually gets married and has children. But all along the Hebrew people he had left behind in slavery were crying out to God to deliver them from the oppression of the Egyptians. Moses spent much of his upbringing in a culture that didn't believe in Jehovah God and now he is returning to a new family which was God-centred.

God steps into the scene

Now Moses was tending the flock of Jethro his father-in-law, the priest of Midian, and he led the flock to the far side of the desert and came to Horeb, the mountain of God. There the angel of the LORD appeared to him in flames of fire from within a bush. Moses saw that though the bush was on fire it did not burn up. So Moses thought, 'I will go over and see this strange sight – why the bush does not burn up.'

> *When the* LORD *saw that he had gone over to look, God called to him from within the bush, 'Moses! Moses!'*
>
> *And Moses said, 'Here I am.'*
>
> *'Do not come any closer,' God said. 'Take off your sandals, for the place where you are standing is holy ground.' Then he said, 'I am the God of your father, the God of Abraham, the God of Isaac and the God of Jacob.' At this, Moses hid his face, because he was afraid to look at God. (Ex. 3:1–6)*

'Moses, Moses' was the sound booming out of a burning bush. He didn't jump, he didn't run, he didn't deny it was him. He answered, 'Here I am'. At that moment it was as if Moses was nailed: he'd been caught. Have you ever had a time when you've wanted to spill the beans but didn't want to face up to going through the process? This was what it must have been like for Moses. Here was an opportunity to get right with God.

Can you imagine the incredible journey of restoration that Moses undertakes – from hiding his face from God in shame, to communicating with God as a friend toward the end of the book. Quite a turnaround. And all of this is achieved through outrageous prayer! Is there anything in your life that seems too difficult for God? Think again! Honesty before God has no boundaries: God wants to know every aspect of our lives intimately. It was no different in the time of Moses as it is now. Don't underestimate how interested God is in you, who you are and what you do.

Whilst Nigel and I were writing this chapter, Nigel admitted that he had cheated at school. I'll let him tell the story:

> *In the third year of secondary school my friend and I were caught cheating in an exam. Not any old exam mind you, it was an RE exam. A teacher, who was a good friend of my*

parents, found us out. He was a man I respected immensely. I really thought I'd blown it big time, partly because I'd cheated and partly because I'd been caught. He ripped into both of us and told us how we had let him down. Yet only two days later he appointed us both as temporary prefects and gave us a second chance. I couldn't believe it at first, but my mood soon changed from shame and anger at myself to thankfulness and relief at his forgiving attitude. In fact, not only had he forgiven us, he'd given us a chance to be responsible and serve the school!

God knew everything Moses had done – he knew where the Egyptian that Moses had killed was buried, and yet he had plans to send him back to Egypt to rescue God's people. Not what Moses had in mind, I'm sure. Moses answers: 'Here I am', and God explains that his people have cried out for deliverance and that Moses is the man for the job. Imagine how he must have felt! I bet his stomach was doing somersaults at that point. He tried four times to get out of the task ahead.

But Moses said to God, 'Who am I, that I should go to Pharaoh and bring the Israelites out of Egypt?' Ex. 3:11

Moses answered, 'What if they do not believe me or listen to me and say, 'The LORD did not appear to you'?' Ex. 4:1

Moses said to the LORD, 'O Lord, I have never been eloquent, neither in the past nor since you have spoken to your servant. I am slow of speech and tongue.' Ex. 4:10

But Moses said, 'O Lord, please send someone else to do it.' Ex. 4:13

How many times have we said something like that to God? What's really crazy is that we pray for opportunities for

God to use us and then when he says OK, we try to get out of it!

> 'We cannot all argue, but we can all pray; we cannot all be leaders but we can all be pleaders; we cannot all be mighty in rhetoric, but we can all be prevalent in prayer. I would sooner see you eloquent with God than with men.'
>
> C.H. Spurgeon, Spurgeon on Prayer and Spiritual Warfare

God knows best

Moses was using any excuse he could – he would have to go back to the city where he was a wanted man, walk into the court of Pharaoh who tried to kill him and be the leader of a people that didn't recognize his authority. Big job ahead, and let's face it, the only way that was going to happen was if Moses was absolutely honest with God, and if God came up trumps with half a dozen miracles.

Moses had at least been honest each time he came up with an excuse. Honest reasons why he shouldn't be the one God chose. But for God, Moses' honesty was a stepping-stone in building one of the greatest stories of breakthrough and deliverance in the Bible: for Moses as a man and for the Israelites as a people. In Exodus 14, in the midst of the mass escape, Moses is standing up in front of everyone saying, 'God's going to part the Red Sea' and within a minute he's crying with worry, and God is reassuring him. Fantastic honesty. Why do we try to hide things from the one person that already knows everything about us?

The bottom line to this story is that if any of us want to develop an outrageous prayer life, we cannot progress without being honest with ourselves and with God. God knows everything – all the dirt we keep hidden, he knows what we are running from and wants to bring us into a depth of relationship with him that we might have never known.

We are really blessed to be able to read the life-stories and experiences of hundreds of people who lived after Moses. We get the inside track on how they overcame sin, what kind of relationship they built with God and how we can develop intimacy with God. Moses didn't have any of this. He didn't have the rest of the Bible to read like we do, but at least he was honest with God about his weaknesses. The good times and bad, he definitely had an open and honest relationship with God.

There are many prompts in the Bible to help us develop in our honesty with God too. We are told that, 'If we confess our sins, he is faithful and just and will forgive us our sins and purify us from all unrighteousness' (1 Jn. 1:9).

Nigel asks: What is 'confession'?

? Confession is to come before God when you pray and to tell him how you feel and the mistakes you might have made. It involves you saying 'I'm sorry'. God knows all this anyway, so what's the point trying to hide or deny it? Let's be honest with him.

Walking in the light is not done by denying sin. It's done by confronting it; allowing God to deal with it and embracing what he has got planned for you. The Greek word for forgive in this verse means to 'dismiss all charges'. So if we want all charges against us to be dismissed, we need to confess them before God. In other words, we are not going to get anywhere by hiding our issues and saying we're not guilty. We are going to get somewhere by confessing our guilt and allowing God to forgive us.

Repentance, like confession, is meant to be from the bottom of your heart. In Acts we read,

'Repent, then, and turn to God, so that your sins may be wiped out, that times of refreshing may come from the Lord' (Acts 3:19).

Repentance is the key to your life being transformed or turned around, refreshed and renewed. Why are we harping on about all this stuff? Well, I don't know of a person alive now or in history that accomplished much in prayer without having a real and honest relationship with God. When they messed up, God was the first person to hear about it. Their prayer life was a reflection of that open relationship. When they prayed, God knew they were absolutely genuine. And when they prayed, they knew that their Heavenly Father had heard the prayer and so they believed the answer was on its way.

Nigel asks: Can you explain 'repentance'?

 When was the last time you said sorry to God for the mistakes you've made? Repentance is wiping the slate clean. Come before God regularly and pray repentantly for anything you may think creates a distance between you and him.

What if I'm not honest?

In Acts 5 Ananias and his wife Sapphira sold some property and gave part of the money to the work of the Kingdom, pretending that it was the full amount. Peter, inspired by the Holy Spirit, challenged Ananias and told him that he was lying. Immediately Ananias fell down dead. A few hours later his wife turned up and tried to carry on with the deception. Peter also challenged her and she dropped down dead too! What is the point in trying to hide stuff from God? It's crazy.

Not surprisingly, the Bible has lots to say about honesty. From dealing or trading dishonestly:

For the LORD *your God detests anyone who does these things, anyone who deals dishonestly. (Deut. 25:16)*

Honest scales and balances are from the LORD; *all the weights in the bag are of his making. (Prov. 16:11)*

To how honesty, or lack of it, will impact every area of your life:

'Make a tree good and its fruit will be good, or make a tree bad and its fruit will be bad, for a tree is recognized by its fruit.' (Mt. 12:33)

'Whoever can be trusted with very little can also be trusted with much, and whoever is dishonest with very little will also be dishonest with much.' (Lk. 16:10)

To the eventual downfall of those who live dishonestly:

The integrity of the upright guides them, but the unfaithful are destroyed by their duplicity. (Prov. 11:3)

The crucial starting point is to be honest with yourself first, 'For by the grace given me I say to every one of you: Do not think of yourself more highly than you ought, but rather think of yourself with sober judgment, in accordance with the measure of faith God has given you' (Rom. 12:3).

Lifestyle not pastime

Honesty before God is a lifestyle not a pastime. One of the biggest mistakes we can make is to have a moment of truth with God and think that we are set up for life. Then within days we can be tempted to hide our actions and feelings from God once again. Think of honesty with God like the times you get together with your mates and you tell them your latest news. We need to act like this in our times of prayer with God – sharing the news, how we feel, our hopes, aspirations and all of the difficulties and pressures we may feel, so that we get to a place where we treat him like the best friend we want him to be.

Often people will ask each other 'How are things?' and the common answer is 'Fine', when the reality is often the opposite – don't be afraid that honesty might be mistaken for moaning. It's better to tell God how you really feel, rather than what we think will impress God.

Moses developed in his relationship with God and had some incredible conversations and prayer times with him:

> Since then, no prophet has risen in Israel like Moses, whom the LORD knew face to face, who did all those miraculous signs and wonders the LORD sent him to do in Egypt – to Pharaoh and to all his officials and to his whole land. For no-one has ever shown the mighty power or performed the awesome deeds that Moses did in the sight of all Israel. (Deut. 34:10–12)

We need to bring ourselves to a place of prayer where we are dependent on God, where we will ask his advice and follow his guidance through Scripture. The subject of honesty is a lifelong pursuit; the first time you're completely honest with God doesn't make you perfect for life. If you make honesty, confession and repentance a lifestyle and keep a short account of sin, then you will place yourself in a good position to operate in a greater depth of prayer.

Nigel asks: I've heard people talk about honesty covenants. What is an 'honesty covenant?'

 This is an agreement between you and God. You are telling God about your intention to live an honest life, and so make a promise (covenant) that you will try and be honest with him in everything you do.

Building trust into your relationship with God will take time and be something that you will have to work at. It is also something that God is likely to test along the way.

My way or God's way

You must remember that God doesn't always play the game by our rules, and he sees life from a heavenly perspective. The Bible tells us that his ways are higher than our ways. Why for example did God harden Pharaoh's heart against Moses and the Israelites time after time? So that his might and supremacy might be displayed (think of the crossing of the Red Sea). I often think that if it was up to us, we would take the easy way out and not see the full extent of the miracle God wants to perform.

Moses had an honesty covenant with God. Eventually he became a trusted friend of God, and a man whose life was dedicated to God's ways. Time and time again he intervened in prayer on behalf of the people by reminding God of the eternal promises he, the Lord, had made. He reached a point where his honest prayers were able to question the heart of God:

The LORD said to Moses, 'How long will these people treat me with contempt? How long will they refuse to believe in me, in spite of all the miraculous signs I have performed among them? I will strike them down with a plague and destroy them, but I will make you into a nation greater and stronger than they.'

Moses said to the LORD, 'Then the Egyptians will hear about it! By your power you brought these people up from among them. And they will tell the inhabitants of this land about it. They have already heard that you, O LORD, are with these people and that you, O LORD, have been seen face to face, that your cloud stays over them, and that you go before them in a pillar of cloud by day and a pillar of fire by night. If you put these people to death all at one time, the nations who have heard this report about you will say, 'The LORD was not able to bring these people into the land he promised them on oath; so he slaughtered them in the desert.'

'Now may the Lord's strength be displayed, just as you have declared: "The LORD is slow to anger, abounding in love and forgiving sin and rebellion. Yet he does not leave the guilty unpunished; he punishes the children for the sin of the fathers to the third and fourth generation." In accordance with your great love, forgive the sin of these people, just as you have pardoned them from the time they left Egypt until now.' (Num. 14:11–19)

Some might argue that Moses was changing God's mind here, but I prefer to think of it as Moses praying in line with God's will. The result was that the people of Israel were saved, and Moses reached an even more intense place in his relationship with God. His prayer was one of the most outrageous of all time – it simply reflected God's will but it also affected the destiny of a nation!

'Prayer is exhaling the spirit of man and inhaling the spirit of God.'

Edwin Keith, www.thinkexist.com

Isn't it time we levelled with God? Today can be the day you decide that a greater depth of honesty is something that becomes part of your life for good. If you want to be honest with God and don't know how to start, why not pray the prayer below and then ask God for guidance from there?

> God I want to be completely honest with you.
> Help me to understand what that means.
> Forgive me for all the times I've not been
> honest in the past. I want my prayer times to
> be the most honest place in my life. I confess
> my faults to you today and want to turn my life
> around and ask you to use my life for your
> Kingdom. Amen.

2 REALIZING YOU ARE A PRODUCT OF SOMEBODY ELSE'S PRAYERS

Prayer shapes lives

Have you ever thought that even last night God might have been waking up hundreds of people in different times zones and countries, burdening those people to pray for you, your circumstance and your future? Just a couple of times in my Christian life, people that I don't know very well have contacted me and said something like, 'I was woken up at 2am last Thursday, and you were very much on my heart; God burdened me to pray this way for you.' Little did they know that at that precise time I was going through the crisis that they explained they were praying for – I have no idea how God does that – but I'm really glad he does!

I spent my childhood faithfully attending a miners' mission chapel in a small village in South Wales, where I had a good grounding of Scripture and met some of the most faithful Christians I have known. Sadly I became distant from God between 1991 and 1993 and moved from that area.

In September of 1993, after much waywardness, I decided to go back to church for a special anniversary service, as I had been invited by a close friend of mine. Like a prodigal coming home, the pastor and everyone there welcomed me back with open arms. But the biggest thing that stuck out that weekend was speaking to one of the old ladies, Irene Turner, who at eighty-four had dedicated the last years of her life to prayer. She said, 'I have prayed for you every day since you have been away and asked the Lord to bring you back to work for him.'

These words penetrated my hard heart, as I was amazed that someone would dedicate herself to pray for me. It was the first realization that my life was becoming a product of someone else's prayer. When I say that, I mean that this was for good in every sense of the word. She only ever wanted what was best for me.

Think about it; how many people over the years – family members, friends, neighbours and people who you might never meet – have prayed for you because God has burdened them? It will be a great time in heaven when strangers tell us stories of when they prayed, even having a vision of what we looked like; they'll be introducing themselves because of a burden they had from God.

Let me illustrate. In his letter to the Romans, Paul briefly mentions some relatives, 'Greet Andronicus and Junias, my relatives who have been in prison with me. They are outstanding among the apostles, and they were in Christ before I was' (Rom. 16:7).

It's the only time in Scripture we hear about these two people. I've often wondered if as his relatives, they would have been praying for Saul (his name before he was saved) when he was busy killing Christians. They must have done some serious spiritual warfare in their prayer times for Paul's life to be so dramatically turned around!

The same can be said of Eunice and Lois, the mother and grandmother of Timothy (who Paul later befriended and travelled with): 'I have been reminded of your sincere faith, which first lived in your grandmother Lois and in your mother Eunice and, I am persuaded, now lives in you also' (2 Tim. 1:5). Paul is reminding Timothy of the heritage of faith in his family and shows Timothy that he should be thankful for it. Can you see the picture forming? Timothy's life has been shaped by the prayer of his immediate family and then Paul. Paul who himself had been influenced by prayer, later goes on to pray for Timothy as he helps him grow in the faith of Jesus Christ.

Nigel asks: What do you mean by 'spiritual warfare'?

This is not Star Wars! Just as earthly combat is the fight between two opposing forces, the spiritual fight of prayer between God and the devil is similar except for one thing – God will always win.

Prayers leave a trail

Have you ever seen a plane flying across a crystal blue sky? It leaves a brilliant white trail behind it. Some mornings in the summer months from where I live you can look at the sky and see hundreds of these lines because I live under the general flight path of aeroplanes flying from Europe to the United States. I've often thought about what prayers would look like if we could see them leaving behind similar trails in the sky. Where did the prayer originate from and where will it land? If only we could see the spiritual realm in this way – like communication lines of intercession, we would be so inspired and encouraged to see the extent of outrageous prayer that already exists for us and around us.

Nigel asks: Explain what you mean by 'the spiritual realm'?

Most of our life exists in the physical realm, but our spiritual experience of God and the fight between good and evil exists in the spiritual realm. We often think that the Kingdom of God is in a place far away, whilst the Bible suggests the Kingdom of God is within us. Engaging with the spiritual realm is more of an attitude of prayer and of heart than going to a physical location.

We live in a nation where only about 7 per cent of the population attend church, but let's not get disheartened. Let's realize that all of the prayers of the Christians in centuries gone by also count. In Hebrews 11 we read of a great cloud of witnesses, men and women of faith who 'did not receive the things promised; they 'welcomed them from a distance' (verse 13). Christians before us may well have finished their lives not seeing everything accomplished that they prayed for, but their hope and desire is that we will now go on to complete some of the burden of God's heart that they also carried.

Most of you reading this will have heard of Selwyn Hughes. He's the author of over 50 Christian books, a world-famous preacher and writes *Every Day with Jesus*. In his autobiography he talks about the day he was taken as a baby to church:

I was named Selwyn, which in Welsh means 'clear voice'. My parents said they gave me this name because they hoped and prayed that I would use my voice in the service of Jesus Christ. The pastor of the mission hall also happened to be my uncle. Some of those present told me years later that as he took me in his arms to pray over me they were surprised when, after finishing his prayer, he paused for a moment and said, 'And Lord I ask that one day you will make this child a preacher of the gospel'.

Over the years, I have often pondered on my uncle's apparent afterthought. Scripture says, 'The prayer of a righteous man is powerful and effective' (James 5:16). Believe me, there was no-one more righteous than my uncle. That godly man, I believe, caught something of God's desire for my life as he held me in his arms and prayed a prayer of dedication that was in harmony with the purposes of God.[1]

Nigel asks: What is 'intercession'?

Prayer is communication between you and God. Intercession is praying what is on God's heart, pleading with him on behalf of someone else.

In the Old Testament Hannah was desperate to have a son, and prayed so earnestly and outrageously that at one point Eli thought she was drunk. She visited the temple frequently and pestered God until he answered her. She promised the Lord that she would be happy to encourage her son into the ministry of the temple under the guidance of Eli:

. . . they brought the boy to Eli, and she said to him, 'As surely as you live, my lord, I am the woman who stood here beside you praying to the LORD. I prayed for this child, and the LORD has granted me what I asked of him. So now I give

him to the LORD. For his whole life he will be given over to the LORD.' (1 Sam. 1:25–27)

Hannah's prayers had been answered and she even gave her son a name to testify to this. The Bible tells us that 'Samuel' means 'because I asked the Lord for him'. Samuel's very existence had been brought about by prayer, and when he had grown up Samuel discovered the privilege of answered prayer in his own experience.

'The greatest gift we can give to others is our prayers.'

Charles Stanley, www.powertopray.com

Jesus prays for Peter – and for you!

Let's turn our attention to the life of Simon Peter and discover what part the prayers of others played in his journey. If you know anything about Peter at all you'll know that he was hot-headed, eager to please, that his enthusiasm sometimes ran away with him, and that at a crucial moment he denied ever knowing Jesus. Yet Peter had one incredible thing going for him. Jesus was praying for him: 'But I have prayed for you, Simon, that your faith may not fail. And when you have turned back, strengthen your brothers' (Lk. 22:32).

This happens towards the end of the Last Supper and in the same conversation Jesus reveals that Peter is going to deny three times that he knows Jesus. Peter is dumbfounded and cannot believe this will happen. In the context of the last chapter about honesty, Peter isn't ready or willing to have an 'honesty moment' before Jesus. But Jesus, knowing Peter's response before he speaks, was actually saying, 'Peter, I know you make mistakes; you are about to make a massive one, but I believe in you. I'm praying for you, and my prayers will help shape your future. You will be a vital person in the life of the early church.' Jesus' words are also fulfilling what was said to Peter on an earlier instance, 'Now I say to you that you are Peter, and upon this rock I will build my church, and all the powers of hell will not conquer it' (Mt. 16:18, NLT).

The prayers and the faith of Jesus helped transform a loud-mouthed coward into a solid rock on which the church was built! As we read through the Acts of the Apostles we see the great transformation in the life of Peter – Jesus' prayer is being lived out; Peter's faith does not fail and he is strengthening his brothers in Christ. Outrageous prayer becomes a key weapon in Peter's armoury. Through prayer he is able to imitate the ministry of Jesus and raise someone from the dead:

> Peter sent them all out of the room; then he got down on his knees and prayed. Turning toward the dead woman, he said, 'Tabitha, get up.' She opened her eyes, and seeing Peter she sat up. He took her by the hand and helped her to her feet. Then he called the believers and the widows and presented her to them alive. This became known all over Joppa, and many people believed in the Lord. (Acts 9:40–42)

For Peter, it wasn't just the prayers of Jesus that helped shape him, it was Jesus' example too. In the incident above Peter acts very similarly to Jesus in Mark 5 when Jesus raises the daughter of Jairus from the dead. Peter would have been there and experienced that, and now he was putting the same thing into practice. The result was again an answer to the prayer of Jesus we have already discovered in Luke 22: as a result of Peter's faith many more became Christians. Peter was strengthening the believers and the church was being built.

You need to be encouraged that Jesus didn't just pray for Peter but he prayed for you too. In John's gospel Jesus prays this:

'My prayer is not for them alone. I pray also for those who will believe in me through their message, that all of them may be one, Father, just as you are in me and I am in you. May they also be in us so that the world may believe that you have sent me. I have given them the glory that you gave me, that they may be one as we are one: I in them and you in me. May they be brought to complete unity to let the world know that you sent me and have loved them even as you have loved me.' (Jn. 17:20–23)

Jesus is praying for every believer that ever lived and ever will live. He is praying for unity, for intimacy with him and with the Father, and for a powerful demonstration of God's love to the world through his followers. This prayer is as effective today as it was then. Jesus first prayed this prayer on earth and it continues to be the burden of his heart now he is in heaven – how awesome is that!

Prayer connects people

Another extremely important event in the life of the early church centred on Peter, and this time God used the prayers of a Roman centurion called Cornelius:

One day at about three in the afternoon he had a vision. He distinctly saw an angel of God, who came to him and said, 'Cornelius!'

Cornelius stared at him in fear. 'What is it, Lord?' he asked.

The angel answered, 'Your prayers and gifts to the poor have come up as a memorial offering before God. Now send men to Joppa to bring back a man named Simon who is called Peter. (Acts 10:3–5)

Cornelius, in obedience to God, sent some of his servants to find Peter, and by the time they arrive where Peter is staying, he has had an incredible vision as a result of his own prayer time:

> *About noon the following day as they were on their journey and approaching the city, Peter went up on the roof to pray. . ..He saw heaven opened and something like a large sheet being let down to earth by its four corners. It contained all kinds of four-footed animals, as well as reptiles of the earth and birds of the air. (Acts 10:9,11–12)*

Through Cornelius and through this strange vision, God uses Peter to bring the good news of Jesus to the Gentiles. Initially, Peter was reluctant and uncertain about this, but with so many different prayers and people involved in this process it was only a matter of time before he grasped the significance of what was happening. A large crowd of Gentiles soon gather around, and after Peter preaches powerfully to them the Holy Spirit comes upon them. After they begin praising God, Peter baptises them and the first Gentile church comes into being.

Don't get the idea that Peter's new found authority meant he didn't need the prayers of others any more. Far from it! In Acts 12, Peter is arrested and thrown into jail by King Herod who intended to bring him out for a public trial. Verse 5 reads, 'But while Peter was in prison, the church prayed very earnestly for him.'

It isn't too long before the prayers of the church are answered. An angel visits Peter in prison and leads him out. Peter is so stunned he thinks it's all a dream. Once again his life has become the product of other people's prayer. The reaction of the church themselves when they discover Peter has been released is an interesting one, which we will come back to in chapter 3.

Towards the end of his life, Peter writes two letters that have become part of the Bible. He writes to give encouragement to Christians who are being persecuted and he writes to warn against false teaching. Read these words from the start of his second letter, and recognize the authority and confidence with which he speaks:

> *This letter is from Simon Peter, a slave and apostle of Jesus Christ. I am writing to all of you who share the same precious faith we have, faith given to us by Jesus Christ, our God and Saviour, who makes us right with God. May God bless you with his special favour and wonderful peace as you come to know Jesus, our God and Lord, better and better. As we know Jesus better, his divine power gives us everything we need for living a godly life. He has called us to receive his own glory and goodness!* (2 Pet. 1:1–3, NLT)

In a very real sense Peter is commencing this letter with a heartfelt prayer for all who read it. It is as if he's determined to make sure that others can be a product of his prayers. He recognizes that all Christians share the same faith in Jesus and he's desperate to see more and more people experience the same fullness of God's power that he has experienced himself.

Ride the wave of prayer

So be encouraged. We've looked at the huge potential in your life that the prayers of others can be. You may have picked up this book looking for answers to situations in your life that you are completely unable to fix. You believe those situations would need an act of God to change. Well, when you begin to develop your prayer life and realize that you are a product of other people's prayer, your perspective changes. Let's face it, when things around you might be going completely wrong, the only thing left to do then is pray. God may step in with a miracle, and you should never believe that he can't do this.

We'll expand this in the next chapter, but I've come to think as I've looked through the Bible hundreds of times, in relation to learning what Scripture teaches about prayer, that when we consider how much heaven backs us up in prayer, one of the most important considerations is to say to God, 'Lord I am willing for my life to be shaped by the prayers of others and am open to my life being used for your Kingdom.' Nigel is going to share with you this great little story:

In 1985 I was a volunteer on Mission to London with the evangelist Luis Palau. Every day I drove up from my flat in Surrey to the QPR football ground and joined with about 30 other young people in the evangelism team. It was a great time, but I had a real problem with money – I didn't have any! Things got to desperation level and I set off one morning with me and my car running on empty. I really didn't know how I was going to get home that evening or get back to the mission the next day. Imagine my surprise when one of the other young guys came up to me and said, 'I've been praying for you this morning, and God told me to give you £10. I've only got £5 on me now which you can have, and I'll owe you another £5 tomorrow.' My car's petrol tank got some fuel and my faith was boosted immensely. It was then that I realized there could be real and tangible blessing resulting from being prayed for by someone else.

Please make sure you understand the concept of being a product of someone else's prayer. It's not some kind of forced trap from heaven that will interfere with your own free will. It is a positive God-filled shaping of life. One way to think of it is to imagine that you are riding the crest of the wave of prayer that people have prayed over time for you, and will continue to pray over the coming months and years. God isn't going to force you into anything, but he will endeavour to line up your desire for him with his destiny for your life over time. In this context, other people's prayer is only ever a huge benefit.

I know that sometimes I've thought I was 'the man', and sought the limelight from ministry and speaking opportunities, but the Lord has reminded me particularly through Scriptures that I am only a product of someone else's prayer. Even in writing this book, it would be easy to slide into a mode of being an expert in prayer, when really I've only got this far in learning how to communicate to God through prayer because of people like Irene Turner who dedicated some time praying for me when I was distant from God. I will be eternally grateful for the times when God has burdened other people to pray for me.

In thinking of a prayer for this section I thought it would be good to at least let God know we want to go deeper with him in prayer.

> **'Lord let me pray what is on your heart – let me go beyond myself and touch the burden of your kingdom. Make my life a prayer and let the words that I utter be a profound influence on the circumstances around me. Lord, help me be a reflection of your grace and a source of your glory, in Jesus' Name. Amen.**

'The power of prayer is like turning on a light as it illuminates God's purpose for our lives. There is no greater connection to knowing His will other than the word.'

Thomas Kinkade, www.presidentialprayerteam.org

3 DEVELOPING A FAITH-FILLED PERSPECTIVE

'Prayer is not only asking, but an attitude of mind which produces the atmosphere in which asking is perfectly natural.'

Oswald Chambers, My Utmost for His Highest

Exercising faith

It wasn't until my very first visit to Uganda in 1996, that I discovered the difference between exercising and not exercising faith in prayer. Faced with needs that only God could answer, I soon understood what it was to exercise faith as we prayed regularly for Aids sufferers, the unemployed and the homeless; believing that God would answer our prayers. The Bible tells us that faith is 'being sure of what we hope for and certain of what we do not see' (Heb. 11:1).

Our mission team for the trip included a precious couple. The wife had severe eyesight problems but was full of faith as she travelled 4500 miles to Uganda to serve God. During our time there we needed all of the team to participate in the ministry time at the end of each meeting when we prayed for people who had responded to the message. In some of the meetings there were upwards of a thousand people asking for prayer. With a team of a dozen people, each team member would end up praying for eighty to a hundred people.

For most of us in the team this was a great challenge and a new experience. Many of us were new to this kind of praying and had never 'stood in the gap' for someone (more of this in chapter 6). As we were praying for these people, we were coming to terms with exercising faith as much, if not more, than the people being prayed for.

The lady on our team with the eye infection met the challenge. I remember one particular meeting where several hundred ladies responded and I felt the Lord suggest to me that this young, nervous team member should be at the forefront of the group praying for people. I cannot explain what happened next more than to say that nearly every single person she prayed for came back the next day to report that the Lord had performed a miracle. Several ladies came forward to testify that they had been haemorrhaging for days, and with no money to see a doctor or get treatment had thought that the only way to get better was to attend church that Sunday and plead with God for a miracle. The faces of those ladies will remain with me forever. The haemorrhaging had stopped, they felt physically better and were radiant with the knowledge that God had come through for them. Our female team member was so blessed that God had used her and that her faith had risen to the occasion. In spite of her own weakness, God had used her.

'All I know is that when I pray, coincidences happen; and when I don't pray, they don't happen.'

Dan Hayes, www.startingwithgod.com

Faith or fear?

Developing a life of faith is definitely a process and in my own experience I've become increasingly confident that my prayers will be answered because of the accumulating evidence that God has answered other prayers before now. Doubt is an enemy of faith – a contradiction that will always stop the flow of faith in prayer.

If you consider the people you meet and the conversations that you have throughout the day, most will agree that our lives are influenced by the media. Over the decades the enemy has so subtly invaded our society that faith has been banished from the far extremities of our heart. As Christians we suffer from this lack of faith. Often we don't believe what we are praying for. I've met countless people and been in many meetings where the lack of faith is almost tangible; where people are bringing circumstances to God almost for the sake of impressing the others in the room that hear them praying, when actually they may have little or no belief in anything they pray.

If we are honest with ourselves we will recognize that many of us carry an outlook on life that isn't spectacular or positive. We conclude that our life will be a victim of a bad news statistic at some point. Statistics say that we're more likely to get cancer than not, that meat, eggs, milk – even water contains things that are likely to make us sick. Our economy is gloomy and it's unlikely to allow us to achieve our ambition or desire. The best that we can hope for is an existence where we might be able to avoid being mugged or attacked. It's almost inevitable that we'll have some kind of major surgery at some point in our lives. The prospect of meeting the right person, getting married, having children without divorce is unheard of – SSSSSSSSTTTTTTTTOOOOOOOOOOOPPPPPP!

It's that kind of doubt and despair that drives faith away. Whatever happened to the knowledge that, 'I can do everything through him who gives me strength' (Phil. 4:13), or 'You, dear children, are from God and have overcome them, because the one who is in you is greater than the one who is in the world' (1 Jn. 4:4)?

Those are mightily powerful and faith-filled verses. When did we so downgrade God in our lives and our society to the place where the power he exercised on the cross to forgive our sins has been separated from our outlook on life? How can we pray with faith for others when we don't believe God can move in our own lives? Today in a world full of uncertainty the message of Christ is so sure; it is a glowing light in darkness. I refuse to end my life having just existed by the skin of my teeth. I am going to make a difference for Jesus; nothing the devil, his demons or evil spirits do will stop that. You might be thinking I've got a little heated about this, and you'd be correct. I'm fed up hearing about what a non-Christian culture tells me is right and acceptable – it's not. If Jesus is the reason for your existence, then let him influence the circumstances around you. Don't let the circumstances influence you.

I was speaking in a church the weekend before writing this chapter, and I'd had a pretty awful week leading up to it. In my quiet times God was asking me if I was going to let him out of the box in the coming year. I was arguing with God and saying things like, 'How dare you say that – I've served you in my life and I've done this for you, I've given you this and done that'. Then God cut to the chase and said, 'When is your life going to revolve around what I'm doing for you more than what you think you are doing for me?' That hit home; God wanted me to serve him at his intended level not at mine, he wanted obedience instead of sacrifice and in many ways I'd tried to serve God on my terms not on his. Ouch.

In my preaching at this church I tried to relate this encounter by using a glass of water: the glass representing my life and the water representing God – and my life was a container full of the Holy Spirit. I confessed that I was happy to hold on to what God had put in my life but not so comfortable sharing it with other people. To make the message hit home I threw the water out of the glass and onto the floor and said, 'When we let God out of our 'box' (the glass) it's impossible to try and contain him again. We can't then say 'come on God, jump back in'; we can't limit God to our expectations when we don't feel like playing the game of faith any longer.'

When we say things like, 'Lord do with me what you will', or 'take me to any part of the world you want' or 'Lord I'll do anything for you', he actually believes us and starts to take us at our word. If you think of the times in your own life when you've said those kinds of things to God, what do you think his response will be? No thanks? Not a bit of it. He's thrilled that we want to serve his Kingdom, but it's on his terms not ours.

'When the devil sees a man or woman who really believes in prayer, who knows how to pray, and who really does pray, and, above all, when he sees a whole church on its face before God in prayer, he 'trembles' as much as he ever did, for he knows that his day in that church or community is at an end.'

R.H. Torrey, www.liftupusa.com/pquotes

Faith-filled prayer is allowing heaven to invade earth through you. For me right now there is a furnace of faith burning inside of me that is screaming out. I want to see the miracles of the Bible active in my life, my home, my street, my town and my nation. I don't want miracles to be consigned to biblical history or a far away country that is in revival; God wants to use you and me in the here and now to be instruments of change for good. Here is a story that Nigel remembers when he experienced friends praying faith-filled prayers for him.

At the end of the first term of my second year at university I faced a big accommodation problem. I was living in a one room flat all on my own and it was pretty desperate. It was cold, draughty, damp, expensive, lonely, and with terrible neighbours above who used to drag a motorbike up the stairs each day. I remember going to the university accommodation office and pleading with them for a room back in a hall of residence for the start of the next term. The accommodation officer told me that I had no chance – there were no vacancies and a long waiting list. That evening I went along to a small group Bible study with some friends as usual, but was really depressed. When it came to sharing prayer needs I mentioned my situation but concentrated more on the fact that I'd been told there was no chance of a place back in a hall. When the leader of the study said they were going to pray for the situation I politely reminded him of the 'no chance' scenario but he started praying anyway. It was the first time I had experienced people praying and believing what they were praying about. They prayed specifically and clearly and prayed with faith. It made me realize that my viewpoint of the situation had been completely faith-less not faith-full. What was the result of the prayer? Two days later I got a note from the accommodation office saying that someone had dropped out of a course, a room had become available and it was being offered to me. It was in exactly the same halls of residence and even the same block, where I already had friends living. Whose faith contributed to this? Not mine I'm afraid to say, but definitely that of the guys and girls in the small group who prayed for me.

Nigel asks: Explain 'thanksgiving' to us.

Wouldn't it be boring never to say thank you to God when he has answered prayer? A prayer of thanksgiving is just that – saying thank you. The good thing is you can pray this type of prayer in advance of God doing something, when you're sure he will answer.

An attitude of gratitude

When was the last time you woke up in the morning with a prayer of thanksgiving on your lips? Nigel says his wife wakes up with a prayer of thanksgiving every morning when she opens her eyes and sees him. Gill is due for an appointment with her optician soon! If you think of all the things that God has done for you even before you knew him, there should be no reason why you are not down on your knees in thanksgiving: 'For I know the plans I have for you,' declares the LORD, 'plans to prosper you and not to harm you, plans to give you hope and a future' (Jer. 29:11).

That should give us an incredible boost of faith, and what about these verses as well:

> Do not be anxious about anything, but in everything, by prayer and petition, with thanksgiving, present your requests to God. (Phil. 4:6)

> I urge, then, first of all, that requests, prayers, intercession and thanksgiving be made for everyone. (1 Tim. 2:1)

> For everything God created is good, and nothing is to be rejected if it is received with thanksgiving. (1 Tim. 4:4)

The Bible clearly shows us how thanksgiving can build up our faith and help us create a positive outlook on life. At this very moment you might feel depressed and negative about your circumstances. Use the verses above to help you understand the power and the freedom and the release that being thankful brings. By the end of today find a Christian friend who will stand alongside you and pray with you that your life will begin to be filled with hope and faith. Pray prayers of thanksgiving together for any good things that come to mind. If you haven't yet got that level of faith, put yourself next to someone who can exercise faith on your behalf.

Nigel asks: What does 'corporate prayer' mean?

Basically it means praying with people. Remember the phrase, 'the whole is greater than the sum of the parts'? This is what corporate prayer is like. Imagine getting two thousand people together that all prayed at the same time – like they do in Korea – that is an example of corporate prayer. There are loads of ways to have a corporate prayer time that you may not have experienced yet – try it out.

Breaking the chains

In many respects the battle of belief we face is very much paralleled by the story of Peter in prison in Acts 12. This is an amazingly honest account of belief gone wrong on all sides, and it's a situation where the Christians are influencing circumstance even though they don't necessarily believe what they are praying for.

Reading through the chapter you get a sense of the scene developing. James, the brother of John, had already been killed for his faith, and that would have sent shock waves through the early church. The disciples would have realized once again that they were in a life or death situation. On the one hand they would have felt extreme pressure but on the other they were prepared to be imprisoned rather than denied the opportunity of sharing their faith. King Herod orders Peter to be arrested and thrown in prison awaiting trial. Then we read this: 'So Peter was kept in prison, but the church was earnestly praying to God for him' (Acts 12:5). The church was gathered to pray for Peter but as the story develops you begin to wonder if they actually expected their prayers to be answered or not.

The night before Peter's trial he was sleeping bound with chains between two guards with another two guards at the door. The room was dark and silent and the only exit was well covered. Even if he could have escaped and gone past the guards there was a huge, locked gate which would have prevented him getting out to the city. Then, incredibly, an angel shows up:

Suddenly an angel of the Lord appeared and a light shone in the cell. He struck Peter on the side and woke him up. 'Quick, get up!' he said, and the chains fell off Peter's wrists.

Then the angel said to him, 'Put on your clothes and sandals.' And Peter did so. 'Wrap your cloak around you and follow me,' the angel told him. Peter followed him out of the prison, but he had no idea that what the angel was doing was happening; he thought he was seeing a vision. They passed the first and second guards and came to the iron gate leading to the city. It opened for them by itself, and they went through it. When they had walked the length of one street, suddenly the angel left him. (Acts 12:7–10)

Peter wasn't even dressed, and had no concept when he got to prison that God was going to do anything. This was the man who had denied Christ three times, yet who was still told by Jesus that he was going to be the building block for the early church. Here he was sharing his faith so much that he'd been sent to jail and he didn't possess a 'get out of jail free' card! This man of faith had spent three and a half years learning from Jesus but was still unprepared for God to perform a miracle. People had been healed just by Peter's shadow (see Acts 5:15), but at this moment he wasn't expecting anything other than to be sitting in jail for a while.

When the angel appears he not only performs the miracle but also explains to Peter what is happening, because not only was Peter uncertain about what was going on, he also thought it was a dream. As they passed by the guards and came to the iron gate, the gate swung open and they were outside. Peter was now as free as a bird; or at least you would think so. In one sense though he was as captive as he was a few minutes before, because he still hadn't fully understood what had occurred. This begs the question; how often do we pray for something to happen or a circumstance to change, when truthfully we doubt that our prayer will be answered? Even when circumstances begin to alter, we don't acknowledge that God might be involved.

Peter and the angel walked slowly down the length of the street like a scene at the end of a film where the two heroes head off into the distance. The angel then hops off to his next assignment and Peter is left trying to make sense of what has just happened. He does finally admit in Acts 12:11 that he knows without a doubt that God sent this angel to help him. He has been unchained, led past the guards, through the iron gate and along the full length of the street – all by a heavenly being, and only then does he recognize that God might just have had a hand in it.

But the scene hasn't finished yet. God has answered the cry of intercession from the church who is meeting in a night of prayer for Peter, and right on cue Peter goes along to the very house where people are meeting to pray for his release. He hammers on the door, and it is the servant Rhoda who comes to see who it is. When she recognizes Peter's voice, she is so overjoyed that she runs back without opening it and exclaims, 'Peter is at the door!' 'You're mad,' they told her. When she kept insisting that it was so, they said, 'It must be his angel.' But Peter kept on knocking and when they opened the door and saw him, they were astonished. (See Acts 12:13–16.)

Just believe

Both Peter and the people praying for his release were genuinely surprised when their prayers were answered. What's more amazing than that is the fact that in spite of all this unbelief God did exactly what they had been praying for. The power of prayer knows no boundaries and can even overcome unbelief and doubt. Jesus spoke of it in this way:

> 'Have faith in God,' Jesus answered. 'I tell you the truth, if anyone says to this mountain, 'Go, throw yourself into the sea,' and does not doubt in his heart but believes that what he says will happen, it will be done for him. Therefore I tell you, whatever you ask for in prayer, believe that you have received it, and it will be yours.' (Mk. 11:22–24)

Here Jesus mentions twice that belief is as important as praying. We need our belief system to be upgraded in order to cope with the potential of God stepping in and actually answering our prayer. Why not put some of this dynamic, belief-filled prayer into practice? You've got nothing to lose. Perhaps you look back on your life and remember many times when you have asked for God's help with a particular worry or problem. You have begged him to step in and sort it out, but you have had a real difficulty leaving that problem at the cross. Mentally you have taken the issue back into your possession and not relied on him for an answer.

Nigel asks: What do you mean by 'leaving things at the foot of the cross'?

We believe that Jesus is the Son of God and that God sent him to earth to deal with sin and to enable us to have a relationship with God. When he died and rose again, he eventually went to sit at the right hand of God the Father, praying for all believers. When we pray we can symbolically bring our prayers to the place where Jesus won the victory and we are handing our worries and concerns over to him.

Getting rid of the baggage

I would like to think however that our part in this is to sort out as much as possible at our end of the deal so that if God is planning to move (and most of the time he does), then we are ready for that to happen. A pastor in a church I used to attend once shared a helpful illustration about this. He said that when most people come to church it's as if they carry an invisible sack on their backs that is filled with bricks. Each brick is labelled with the sin issues that the people have and the accusations people have made against them, or even the fears and feelings of guilt that they carry. They enter into a godly environment and have a great opportunity to lay their bag full of bricks at the cross and not to pick it up again when they leave. But people have become so familiar with bags of bricks in their lives that those bags become more real than the potential of the miracle that removes the bags. I thought this was an excellent illustration and in my own life made every effort to come before God each time I was in church and try to deal with one of the bricks in the bag I was carrying around.

You could begin to do that now. Take the issue to God and trust him to carry the load. Then when Satan tries to persuade you that your life exists only with this specific problem, remind yourself of what you have asked God for and the fact that God answers prayer.

There is no point in trying to develop a fantastic prayer life if you don't believe that much of what you pray will become a reality. If you have trouble believing that God could really answer your prayers, then slow things down a bit and work at some basics. Ask God to help you with your belief for answered prayer. Ask God to show you some of the concerns that are on his heart to pray: then you will be partnering with him in prayer!

'Remember that you can pray any time, anywhere. Washing dishes, digging ditches, working in the office, in the shop, on the athletic field, even in prison – you can pray and know God hears!'
Billy Graham, www.calvarychapel.com

Lord, help me to pray prayers of faith, and help me to believe that you answer prayer. Help me to develop a faith-filled perspective in my prayers. I ask this in the name of Jesus, Amen.

4 PRAYING THE PRAYERS THAT ARE ON GOD'S HEART

'Prayer is not overcoming God's reluctance, but laying hold of His willingness.'

Martin Luther, from a speech 'Been to the Mountain'

God's heart

At the time of writing a tsunami has devastated the coasts of several nations in the Bay of Bengal extending into the rest of the Indian Ocean – to Indonesia, Thailand, Sri Lanka and as far as the east coast of Africa. The scenes of devastation on the television were traumatic to watch even from several thousand miles away. What made this all the more poignant was the fact that I've been working with a ministry team for the last several years that has recently started a project in Tamil Nadu, a region in India affected by the tsunami. Two villages in particular where the ministry had been intending to develop a school and a medical clinic have lost 40 per cent of their population. I don't know why God allows things like this to happen. Newspaper reports and insurance companies call a disaster like this an 'Act of God', but that is misleading – God doesn't intend for massive suffering like that to occur. Yet I have wondered what was going on in the heart of God the Father, when hundreds and thousands of people were so severely affected by this natural disaster.

We live in a world of instant international communication: reports on a disaster reach us quicker than relief agencies are able to respond. Yet can you imagine what runs through the mind of a loving God who feels the pain and deep devastation of his creation, whether they believe in him or not? Micro-seconds after the tidal wave hit, he felt the loss, the anguish, the confusion and the pain of those people. Moments later the believers who were lost to the nations involved, ascended to heaven. Their momentary pain was replaced with an eternal peace.

Seeing things from God's perspective and not from ours allows us to appreciate in simple terms the complex nature of our world. Often we are so baffled by trying to understand things beyond our comprehension. God is able to take in and process every thought, prayer, cry of pain and aspiration of every human being on the planet simultaneously – the Bible says that he knows every hair on our head, that we are more important than the sparrows. Yet we also read that God says: 'For my thoughts are not your thoughts, neither are your ways my ways,' declares the LORD. 'As the heavens are higher than the earth, so are my ways higher than your ways and my thoughts than your thoughts' (Is. 55:8–9).

But sometimes we do try to second-guess God and try to twist his arm so he will agree to everything we pray for. In chapter 2 we said that prayer was communicating with God and intercession was praying what was on God's heart. So let's press into this concept a little and see if we can embrace the need of others in a selfless way by discovering what is on God's heart.

I read an article recently in a magazine that listed the ten most altruistic people on the planet (people who had massive wealth and I mean in the billions not the millions). They had decided to make a difference with their money. Between them they had given away something like 45 billion pounds and were still giving away more. They were pumping more money than it takes to run a small country into the charities they believed in. For some it was the eradication of disease, for others it was providing homes for tens of thousands of children. Others provided schooling and funded university students whilst others simply supported the propagation of religious faith. An heir to the McDonald's food chain gave over 1 billion dollars to the Salvation Army in the United States.

I mention all this because each of these generous givers demonstrated that their belief system steered the way in which they used their resources. They could have left their money in the bank, gaining more annual interest than you or I would have in our accounts over a lifetime, but what set this group apart was their determination to bring change to a world that desperately needed it.

'To pray is to change. Prayer is the central avenue God uses to transform us.'
Richard Foster, Celebration of Discipline

God's will

Imagine the changes that God brings about each day, when millions of his people pray the burden of his heart. There's some kind of overriding spiritual rule of heaven that God requires his children to pray in order to act – it's the difference between his sovereign and permissive will. Let me explain.

God's sovereign will brings change when it hasn't been asked for – when he feels strongly enough about something that he acts, simply because he's God. His permissive will however works from the basis of prayer that has been prayed. When Christians all over the world are led to pray for change and God acts, the only thing that we have to remember is that it's change on God's terms not ours.

Often we are guilty of expecting God to answer our prayers like a microwave cooks dinner – fast. We want our prayers answered in a way that is easy and makes us look good, with lots of praise and absolutely zero inconvenience. Imagine coming to God with a prayer request and then setting loads of ridiculous boundaries for the answer: sorry, you can't answer this prayer on Tuesdays or Thursdays, Saturdays are out as I have a lie in, and if you're going to answer prayer on a Sunday, could you possibly do it in between the omnibus edition of EastEnders and when I go to church in the evening.

If that's you then GET A LIFE. Since when did you think you could dictate terms to Almighty God? It's like this: if you have told God you're available, that you want him to use you, and that you'll do anything and go anywhere then he believes you. When he sees your attempts to compromise what you once prayed, or hears you giving him a list of conditions for your prayers to be answered, he must smile gently in heaven and move on. Why on earth would he entrust us to pray what is on his heart when we aren't serious about the prayers we bring to him, especially when he wants to answer those prayers on his terms?

The permissive will of God includes prayer burdens, but I've come to the conclusion that God so desires our involvement in the whole process of bringing an answer, that to him the journey to the answer is as important as the answer itself.

Praying the prayers that are on God's heart involves a process – in my own experience I have realized that he tests us with small burdens before trusting us with bigger ones. Imagine God is speaking and these are the questions he's asking:

- Does this person love me enough to want to receive my burden?
- Is this person honest in their prayers with me?

- How do they react when I work outside of their understanding of time?
- Will they keep the burden in confidence and do they have integrity?

Nigel asks: What is a 'burden'?

A prayer burden is being open and available enough to God to allow him to burden your heart with something he wants prayed for – you might find yourself waking in the early hours of the morning with an urgent need to pray for a particular person or situation.

As these questions indicate, God is definitely interested in our character development in the process of allowing us to receive prayer burdens. We have to understand that having a prayer burden is very rarely for our benefit, it's usually always for other people. If you are selfish to the core, and not interested in anyone else except you, why would God entrust you with the privilege of spending time praying for someone or something else?

Praying a burden

There are lots of instances in the Bible of people praying the burden of God's heart for others. In the book of Daniel we read that this prophet had some understanding of the spiritual attack against his nation and undertakes a season of intense prayer and fasting pleading with God to intervene:

I, Daniel, understood from the Scriptures, according to the word of the LORD given to Jeremiah the prophet, that the desolation of Jerusalem would last seventy years. So I turned to the Lord God and pleaded with him in prayer and petition, in fasting, and in sackcloth and ashes (Dan. 9:2–3).

Daniel was getting a strong sense of God's own heart and he began to do that by searching the Scripture. In his book, *Releasing the Ability of God through Prayer,* Charles Capps details an important attitude to prayer that he sums up as 'praying the answer and not the problem'. He notices that so many people use prayer simply to pour out a problem to God:

Prayer is not telling God your problem. Jesus said, Your Father knoweth what things ye have need of, before ye ask him (Matt. 6:8). For years I thought to pray was to tell God the problem. No, that is not prayer. Telling God the problem is complaining.[2]

Instead Capps says that prayer should be about praying in faith for the answer:

We could sum it up by saying that prayer is not telling God the problem. Whatever you desire is what you should pray, not the problem. Turn loose of the problem. Take hold of the answer and make it your prayer and your confession of faith.[3]

He says that if you pray prayers based on Scripture, you will be praying the prayers that are on God's heart, and you will be praying the answer instead of just praying about the problem! This is because God's word reflects God's heart, and when we pray in accordance with Scripture, we realize that's what we want – we want to discover what is the very best for us –

Hearing your own voice speak God's Word will excite your heart to action.[4]

Daniel discovered this and his prayers began in Scripture, and although he did touch on the problem by confessing his own sins and the sins of the nation, he prayed much more about the answer.

Nigel asks: What do you mean by 'praying Scripture'?

Scripture is incredible. It records the experiences of hundreds of individuals and their relationship with God – what better place to learn from than the Bible! I often find myself praying the prayers of David in the Psalms when I feel a bit down and also praying prayers of breakthrough in the style Paul did in the New Testament when I have felt determined in prayer.

Just read this powerful and heartfelt prayer of Daniel's. It is long but it's worth it.

I prayed to the LORD my God and confessed:
   'O Lord, the great and awesome God, who keeps his covenant of love with all who love him and obey his commands, we have sinned and done wrong. . .We have not listened to your servants the prophets, who spoke in your name to our kings, our princes and our fathers, and to all the people of the land.
   'Lord, you are righteous, but this day we are covered with shame – the men of Judah and people of Jerusalem and all Israel, both near and far, in all the countries where you have scattered us because of our unfaithfulness to you. O LORD, we and our kings, our princes and our fathers are covered with

shame because we have sinned against you. The Lord our God is merciful and forgiving, even though we have rebelled against him; we have not obeyed the LORD our God or kept the laws he gave us through his servants the prophets. All Israel has transgressed your law and turned away, refusing to obey you.

'Therefore the curses and sworn judgments written in the Law of Moses, the servant of God, have been poured out on us, because we have sinned against you.

'. . .Just as it is written in the Law of Moses, all this disaster has come upon us, yet we have not sought the favour of the LORD our God by turning from our sins and giving attention to your truth. The LORD did not hesitate to bring the disaster upon us, for the LORD our God is righteous in everything he does; yet we have not obeyed him.

'Now, O Lord our God, who brought your people out of Egypt with a mighty hand and who made for yourself a name that endures to this day, we have sinned, we have done wrong.

'O Lord, in keeping with all your righteous acts, turn away your anger and your wrath from Jerusalem, your city, your holy hill. Our sins and the iniquities of our fathers have made Jerusalem and your people an object of scorn to all those around us.

'Now, our God, hear the prayers and petitions of your servant. For your sake, O Lord, look with favour on your desolate sanctuary. Give ear, O God, and hear; open your eyes and see the desolation of the city that bears your Name. We do not make requests of you because we are righteous, but because of your great mercy. O Lord, listen! O Lord, forgive! O Lord, hear and act! For your sake, O my God, do not delay, because your city and your people bear your Name.' (Dan. 9:4–11, 13–19)

As we read on we see that before Daniel finishes his prayer God responds: Daniel is visited by Gabriel, one of

God's angels. Daniel 9–10 describes a spiritual battle that the angels of God eventually win. There was a cost however as Daniel prayed so earnestly and in such a determined way that he became extremely weak. In fact the angel had to lay hands on Daniel to restore his strength. This is an amazing scene and just goes to show how much God wants us involved in the process of breakthrough. When we get a prayer burden from God, we need to realize that he sees the answer as a partnership between heaven and earth.

God gives you the burden of his heart

So how do you know when God is burdening your heart? A healthy sign is when you are in bed at night fast asleep and wham – you are wide awake, sitting up in bed, with your heart pounding and your mind filled with the thoughts of a friend who you believe to be in need – that's a prayer burden. You are immediately praying that God would be near the friend, support him or her and work out the situation, whatever it may be. Half an hour or so later the urgency subsides and within moments you're back in the land of nod. Or you may be on the way to school or work and you can't seem to shrug off the idea that a person is in trouble, and right where you are you bring them before the Lord in prayer.

As your journey of availability to pray what is on God's heart goes on, you begin to get an inside look from heaven's perspective on what is happening in people's lives. You might be absolutely consumed over a few weeks to pray for a couple that you believe are having a marriage problem – they have never said anything, and you'll never advertise the fact, but as you trust that what you are receiving is a spiritual insight from God, you will begin to realize that your life is being given seasons of true intercession.

Another biblical example is Noah. He built a massive boat when he'd never seen a boat before; he believed that rains would bring a massive flood when he'd never experienced that before. All the local people thought he was mad, and ridiculed him for trusting with someone they could not see. What possessed Noah to act in this way? It was because God had spoken to him and that was good enough for Noah. He had a close relationship with God and it had grown so strong that Noah believed in what God had spoken to him more than the physical circumstances around him.

Noah's faith was in direct contrast to the rest of the people who were running away from God. Anyhow the story goes that Noah completed the building of the ark and nobody wanted to get onboard. Noah's family were saved and no doubt the people started to have second thoughts about the whole thing when the rain came – so much rain in fact that the ark was the only place of refuge. Noah had heard and physically acted upon the instructions God had given him. He lived out the prayers on God's heart. (You can read about this in Genesis 7–8.)

'Prayer at its highest is a two-way conversation and for me the most important part is listening to God's replies.'

Frank C. Laubach, www.retirementwithapurpose.com

What can we learn from Noah? That we need to develop a kind of Noah perspective in our relationship with God. In prayer terms it might mean being burdened to pray for a particular person, and then after clearing it with God, discreetly contacting the person to see how they are doing – explaining to them how God has burdened your heart to pray for them. I often think of this in terms of an imaginary 'prayer radar': God reveals a situation, or several at a time, which I pray for until they are no longer visible on the radar.

I devote about five to six hours a week to this kind of prayer usually, and then increase the amount of time depending on the urgency of the situation. I cannot tell you the number of times I've contacted the people I've prayed for and explained what it was the Lord highlighted. Many people have been in tears, not knowing which way to turn, but so appreciated the prayer and the support through a phone call or meeting. Please understand that I'm not setting myself up as an expert, because if I'm honest I find the burden of this kind of praying really challenging and often heartbreaking. What I am saying though, is that I know the burden comes regularly when I'm open with God and available to pray this way. There are times when my life gets a bit crowded with other things, and so the prayer burdens decrease. Then when I make more room for God again, within a few days new prayer burdens begin appearing on the 'spiritual radar'.

I don't lock myself away to pray but I often wake up in the morning a little early and just lay in bed for an hour or so and ask God if there are concerns I should be praying for. Some mornings I don't end up praying for anything, other mornings it's very busy. Or I might be on a train or in the car and have time to spare, so I devote that time to the Lord in prayer, not with my requests but his requests, opening up time to selflessly pray for others. My experience is that true intercession doesn't have the words 'bless me' involved at all. There have been crazy times where I've felt the Lord ask me to pray for someone who I haven't met before and then months later I meet the person in the flesh – a bit scary, and I don't even begin to ask God how he does that – but it's really cool!

Praying the prayers of God's heart requires discipline and time and it will definitely test your character. The enemy does have ways of trying to hold the process up; making our lives really busy, or making us feel tired as soon as we try to pray; getting our minds distracted when we read the Bible, but the process involves working through that until we feel the burden lift.

The Celtic Christians used to describe times of prayer when God was really burdening their hearts as 'thin place' times – when heaven and earth seemed unusually close together. During those seasons they would spend a lot of time worshipping and praying to God for his will to come down onto their own nations, for God's Kingdom to be more prevalent on earth.

Go fast!

So what happens if the burden seems overwhelming or doesn't seem to lift after a few days? Well, feeling overwhelmed is not such a bad place to be. Remember that you can't bring the answer, but you are helping the answer arrive. Ultimately it is God who is in control.

I want to ask if you've ever tried fasting. Now don't close the book and throw it across the floor. Fasting should be as much of our Christian walk as the burden of prayer from God itself. There are lots of types of fasting in the Bible. The normal type that most Christians know about is the abstinence of food: missing a meal and using that time in determined prayer with God. Fasting usually brings a sense of focus to you as you pray and definitely suggests to God that you are absolutely serious about what you are praying for. Here's a story from Nigel about discovering the heart of God through fasting.

A few years ago those of us working for Ignite embarked on our first ever UK tour, with a real rock 'n' roll tour bus, lighting rig and sound system. A few months before I had been given a copy of a book about prayer and fasting, and a while before the tour I randomly picked the book up and started reading. Before too long, the Lord convicted me that I should start a fast. I'd fasted before, but I knew this one was going to be different. I had no idea how long I was going to fast but knew that it would be a time of humility before God and a time of personal preparation for Ignite and our tour.

I felt excited about all this, but after a few days was still uncertain how long the Lord was calling me to fast for. Reading on in the book I came to a chapter about 40 day fasts. Immediately I knew that God was calling me to fast for 40 days. I remembered the exact day I had started and worked out 40 days forward in my diary. Imagine my surprise and excitement when this turned out to be the final day of our UK tour! I went into that tour physically weak and tired but spiritually prepared to speak each night to the crowd of young people in each venue. We saw teenagers becoming Christians; many signed up to the Ignite declaration, and there was a real sense of unity in our team. We even ministered to our tour bus driver, an ex-cocaine addict who later gave his life to Jesus. Was that all as a result of my fast? It must have helped – but it's not all about me, rather it is about the fact that God was aligning my life closer to his, and that his purposes were coming through.

Nigel asks: Explain 'fasting' to us.

This is when prayer gets really serious – people deciding to give up something in order to spend a focused time in prayer, and showing God how determined they are for an answer. Fasting is often giving up food, but it could be sacrificing something else such as TV, chocolate, crisps etc.

Fasting in the Bible

In the Bible we often read of God's people fasting because there is a serious need, a desperate cry for an answer from God or a crisis that needs answering. The prophet Ezra reaches a crisis moment when he is preparing to lead a group of exiles back to Jerusalem from captivity in Babylon. This is how he describes the situation:

There, by the Ahava Canal, I proclaimed a fast, so that we might humble ourselves before our God and ask him for a safe journey for us and our children, with all our possessions. I was ashamed to ask the king for soldiers and horsemen to protect us from enemies on the road, because we had told the king, 'The gracious hand of our God is on everyone who looks to him, but his great anger is against all who forsake him.' So we fasted and petitioned our God about this, and he answered our prayer. (Ezra 8:21–23)

In another example, Esther wants to seize the opportunity to speak to her husband, the King of Persia, in order to save her people the Jews. There were two problems however: she'd kept her Jewish nationality a secret, and she couldn't get an audience with the King without being invited. In her moment of decision, Esther gives her uncle Mordecai the following instructions:

'Go, gather together all the Jews who are in Susa, and fast for me. Do not eat or drink for three days, night or day. I and my maids will fast as you do. When this is done, I will go to the king, even though it is against the law. And if I perish, I perish' (Esth. 4:16).

What is the link between Ezra and Esther? Both are in hot water and recognize that fasting will be the key in order to see breakthrough and get closer to God's answers. For most of us, God may not require us to fast, but on occasions we may feel a prompting from deep within us to take the burden of prayer a step further by fasting. There are extreme cases in history, such as the story of Rees Howells who was a famous Welsh prayer figure in the early part of the twentieth century. When taking on the prayer burden of a friend who was suffering from tuberculosis, Howells reduced his food intake to one bowl of soup and bread roll a day for many months, while praying through the burden. His friend got well and interestingly Howells said that he felt the symptoms of the disease himself at one point. This suggested that he had reached a place in prayer where his fervency acted like a wedge between his friend and the disease.

This isn't to say that we should all follow his example! Remember that fasting is something between you and God, not you and anyone you meet! If you are thinking about fasting, please do seek advice. Don't fast from food if you are on medication or have a medical condition. We've put some guidelines on fasting in the appendix at the back of this book, which you may find helpful. It's also a good idea to have a friend or someone you look up to spiritually to keep an eye on you while you fast to make sure you are not going too far by being over-enthusiastic.

If you've read this and still don't feel confident about fasting from food, then why not start with something else, but again only if God is taking you there. Some people I know love chocolate and the thought of giving that up is as bad as not eating at all. Others might love playing computer games or watching television. God will receive the fasting of anything if your heart and motivation is right and it is a real sacrifice.

Father Daniel Nash was a prayer warrior who used to travel ahead of Charles Finney, the great American evangelist, and visit the next town that Finney was due to preach at. Nash would find a small place to stay and then pray for a spiritual breakthrough in that town so that when

Finney would come, people would be saved. He did this for many years and Finney often wouldn't move from the town where he was preaching until Daniel Nash sent him word that everything was prayed through and ready for Finney's visit. Nash would often undertake a total fast and only drink water for several days in order to find the victory in his prayer time. His experience over the years meant that he would quickly gain the burden of God's heart for a town and wrestle with the dark forces that had kept the gospel from that place. He often found that he was prevailing in prayer, which is the final point in this chapter. Prevailing in prayer is a huge part of this jigsaw puzzle of igniting outrageous prayer. It will take your prayer life and experience into the realm of the miraculous – prevailing prayer does not play by the rules and laws of earth, but the rules and laws of heaven.

Nigel asks: What do you mean by 'prevailing'?

Prevailing is like the final push in a race to get to the line – that burst of determination that gets you home. At this point you'll already have had the burden, will have been interceding and are refusing to give up – no matter what the circumstance – until you've seen the answer come.

Going deeper

Daniel Nash and Finney once described a situation that occurred which was bringing distraction to Finney's preaching:

> *Charles Finney could always go to Brother Nash when an obstacle arose in the meetings. One such occasion occurred. . . . where 'some young men seemed to stand like a bulwark in the way of the progress of the work.' In this state of*

things, Brother Nash and myself (Finney), after
consultation, made up our minds that the thing must be
overcome by prayer, and that it could not be reached in any
other way. We therefore retired to a grove and gave
ourselves to prayer until we prevailed, and we felt confident
that no power which earth or Hell could interpose, would
be allowed permanently to stop the revival.[5]

Prevailing in prayer is not some game you can enter on the
last round, it's not a boxing match with one boxer
competing until the tenth round to be replaced by a fresh
competitor. If you want to prevail in prayer it will cost and
cost big time – you might lose friends, you might have to
separate yourself from doing the things you like; you
might even end up walking with a limp like Jacob did
when he wrestled with an angel. You have to start from
round one and work your way up from there, then in the
closing stages of the fight, you start to deliver the final
heaven-backed blows to the enemy, proving that the
weight of the glory of God and the full resources of heaven
back up everything you speak out in prayer. You are at that
point completely submitting to God's will and you reach a
place where his glory in the situation is so tangible you can
only imagine your experience has brought you close to the
reality of what it will be like in heaven.

I remember on a visit to South Africa being in a meeting
where an old man by the name of Pastor Steve Constance
was speaking. I'll come to what he was speaking about in a
moment, but my first experience of him was when he
walked straight through the reception of this two
thousand seat church. He walked past the administration
offices and on into the secretary's office, and then finally
unannounced, opened the door of the pastor's office, who
at the time was on the telephone. I was sitting reading
something just feet away.

Pastor Steve was the only person I knew that had the kind of relationship that over-rode any structure or protocol in the church, such was his standing with church leaders in South Africa. Without saying anything he picked the telephone out of the hand of the pastor – said to the person on the line 'he'll phone you back', put the phone down and then said 'let's pray'. Within moments the presence of the Holy Spirit was so strong in that room – I thought Jesus would show up any minute. Steve took to the platform as the speaker that night and said, 'Friends I'm not going to preach this evening, but we are going to pray for our currency, the rand.' The currency had for months been sliding on world markets and he said he had received a burden from God to get people to pray that it would recover.

Again, I have rarely heard anyone lead prayer like that. Two thousand people for over half an hour were crying out to God to intervene specifically for the currency of their nation. I sensed that the answer was on its way whilst we were still praying; such was the tangible presence of God. Within a few weeks the rand had recovered and today stands stronger than it has for the last 30 years. Coincidence – I don't think so!

Sounds great doesn't it – you can change the destiny of nations with this kind of partnership of prayer. Personally I don't believe everyone is destined to this level of prayer, and even those that are aren't all the time. Just imagine; everything would grind to a halt: no trains running, no bread in the bakery and no TV on air because prevailing prayer is far too consuming. For the few that make it to that level you will see an incredible sense of servanthood being displayed in them; they never take offence and cannot comprehend doing anything to jeopardise someone's walk or relationship with God. The Kingdom of God oozes out of them and they speak with words that describe the potential in everything.

When we begin to align ourselves with the prayers that are on God's heart, we are giving up the right to moan and groan about how bad things are for us. What tends to happen is that we reach a place where we are taking care of God's business, and he usually ends up taking care of our business for us.

> 'Prayer lays hold of God's plan and becomes the link between His will and its accomplishment on earth. . .Amazing things happen and we are given the privilege of being the channels of the Holy Spirit's prayer.'
>
> Elisabeth Elliot, www.retirementwithapurpose.com

God's heart and you

As we finish this chapter you may be overwhelmed by the prospect of praying the prayers of God's heart and you may be feeling totally inadequate for the task. Perhaps you feel unworthy, sinful, aware of previous failures and you imagine that to pray in this way you will need to be a perfect, super-Christian. Well be encouraged by this. The Bible tells us that God says David was 'a man after my own heart' (see 1 Samuel 13:14 and Acts 13:22). David did much to justify this tribute – he defeated a giant, overcame adversity to become King, was a mighty leader in battle, wrote Psalms of praise and worship to the Lord – and even Jesus is called 'the son of David'. Yet David was often arrogant and bad-tempered; he schemed to kill Uriah the Hittite and committed adultery with Uriah's wife Bathsheba. Many of his Psalms are full of repentance and remorse and doubt. David had many flaws and was far from perfect. Yet he most definitely was a person after God's own heart. *The Message* describes David as a man whose heart beats to God's heart. Be encouraged – your heart can begin to beat in tune with God's own heart too. Let's start that process with a prayer.

> **Lord, you know the condition of my heart and I come to you completely open and honest today. I ask you to teach me how to pray the prayers that are on your heart and lead me to a place where I can have the same love and compassion for your people as you do. I want to go deeper in my prayer life with you. Amen.**

5 MAKING PROCLAMATIONS AND DECLARATIONS

'I believe in definite prayer. Abraham prayed for Sodom. Moses interceded for the children of Israel. How often our prayers go all around the world, without real definite asking for anything! And often, when we do ask, we don't expect anything. Many people would be surprised if God did answer their prayers.'

D.L. Moody, Golden Counsels

Childlike faith

I remember once watching one of those spoof movies. It featured a group of muggers standing next to an ATM machine. As each customer would come to use the machine, the mugger would tap them on their shoulder just as they had retrieved their cash and say something like, 'Hi, my name is Jason, I'll be your mugger today' and then take the cash out of their hand. The victim would smile, like it was supposed to happen, and walk away. That scene was supposed to highlight how normal a robbing offence had become in our society and how many of us were resigned to this happening at some point in our lives. As crazy as it sounds, sometimes that is our view of how the enemy works. It is becoming less and less common these days for Christians to expect a positive outcome to difficult situations.

I remember hearing a story where a young boy was nagging his father to take him for a burger. Making up an excuse because he didn't really feel like going, the father told the child that he had a headache. In childlike faith and simplicity the son raised his hand and put it on his father's head saying, 'Lord Jesus, please heal my daddy's head, Amen', and then immediately turned to his father and said, 'Come on then dad, let's go'. He saw a problem, prayed in faith and walked in the belief of an answer. Oh God, let my faith in prayer be like that of the child. If we are willing to take what the Bible says about faith and prayer literally, then we will be amazed at the transformation in our prayer life. One of the best portions of Scripture relating to this is in Mark 11 where we are given instructions about speaking out in faith when we are in difficult situations or face seemingly unmovable problems:

> 'Have faith in God,' Jesus answered. 'I tell you the truth, if anyone says to this mountain, 'Go, throw yourself into the sea,' and does not doubt in his heart but believes that what he says will happen, it will be done for him. Therefore I tell you, whatever you ask for in prayer, believe that you have received it, and it will be yours. And when you stand praying, if you hold anything against anyone, forgive him, so that your Father in heaven may forgive you your sins.' (Mk. 11:22–25)

Twice in this short passage Jesus as much as says 'I'm telling you!' and in some translations he says, 'Listen to me!' In other words, he really wants to catch the disciples' attention and make sure they realize he is speaking real words of truth and wisdom that they need to take hold of. Even though they have been his close followers, they have been uncertain of this amazing fact: that the spiritual realm is far more powerful than the physical realm. Our job two thousand years later is also to believe that what Jesus taught is true, and to adopt it as a principle of

Christian living rather than a temporary state of mind. Forgiveness plays a part too, and we'll look at that later in the chapter.

I've often been challenged to think how God views my problems from a heavenly perspective. The boundary of time is removed because God doesn't work from a clock or a calendar. There isn't financial constraint because God doesn't use currency. There is no barrier of language because everyone understands each other in heaven. There isn't any sickness because everyone in heaven has been made whole. When we look at the heavenly perspective rather than the earthly one, our prayers should be so much stronger and confident. The Bible speaks much about the promises that we have as a result of our faith in Jesus Christ. Of his own miracles, Jesus actually said:

'I tell you the truth, anyone who has faith in me will do what I have been doing. He will do even greater things than these, because I am going to the Father' (Jn. 14:12).

What an outrageous statement. Imagine that! Jesus is telling his followers that because of his death and resurrection, and his return to the Father, anyone who has faith in him will do even greater things than he's done. The apostle Paul picks up on a similar faith-filled and outrageous theme when he says, 'In all these things we are more than conquerors through him who loved us' (Rom. 8:37) and again, 'I can do everything through him who gives me strength' (Phil. 4:13).

All of the above verses suggest that we can tap into the very same power that Jesus had. When the Holy Spirit lives in us, it means that the same power that raised Jesus from the dead is ready and waiting for us to call on a regular basis. Yet so often we don't engage in a spiritual battle because we don't realize God's power is available to us. The physical evidence of a life without spiritual battles is obvious; we submit to every little thing the devil and his demons throw at us. If we all took time to seriously analyse the roots of our worries, stresses and fears, we would find that most of them are driven by a lie or falsehood that is designed by the enemy to stop us reaching our full potential.

What we need is honesty. Before we begin to think about praying declarations and proclamations, we must face up to the fact that most of the time we act like Jesus didn't rise from the dead. We have accepted our intellect as a more real aid to get us through life and have failed to recognize the power of a Saviour who sacrificed his life for us.

Faith for the future

Nigel often talks about his belief that in the UK, and especially Wales where we both live, churches have accepted what he calls 'the law of diminishing generational return'. That's a bit of a mouthful isn't it, but what he means is that each generation has gradually diluted the power and presence of God in their lives and accepted that their children will see less of a move of God than they did. The result is that after four or five generations of this we now live in a society that has compromised its faith in God and has tried to replace the comfort that God brings with the pursuit of wealth and knowledge.

Don't forget that we live in a nation that for centuries placed God at the centre of everything, taking Christianity to many nations in the world. Nigel and I believe that the Bible tells us that each generation should be seeing a greater move of God than the generation before. If we allow God to demonstrate himself through the expression of our faith in him and our desire to serve him, then there will be a dramatic and remarkable change in the way that this whole nation knows and serves God.

Having got all that off my chest let me return to an important question. Which is more real – the physical realm or the spiritual? We defined the spiritual realm in chapter 2 but here is some further insight for you:

- The spiritual realm was around long before the physical
  We see this in the story of creation (Genesis 1).
- Humans were created in the image of God
  We are made up of three components: body, soul (mind or intellect) and spirit.
- The devil's desire is to hide or mask the spiritual realm
  The devil is an expert in influencing the physical. If we were more aware of the spiritual realm, we would be more ready for spiritual warfare.

Our motivation should not be just to gain knowledge of the spiritual place, but to fall more in love with Jesus. This puts us in a place of surrendering to his will for our life. When this happens we become more attuned to the interaction between the two realms.

'When God speaks, oftentimes His voice will call for an act of courage on our part.'

Charles Stanley, www.retirementwithapurpose.com

Changing a nation

It's time to give you examples of what I'm talking about. I remember hearing the story told by a pastor called John Mulinde who was talking about the spiritual turnaround in Uganda. John was describing what it was like to live in a country that was ruled by a dictator called Idi Amin. There was oppression and the killing of Christians, and the whole country suffered from the lack of basic human needs such as food and housing. The Christian church used to meet in secret for fear of being caught by the police. Could you live as a follower of Jesus in a country where Christianity had been banned?

Christian leaders began to meet together to pray. Millions simply accepted that Idi Amin's evil plans would permanently change Uganda for the worst, but a couple of hundred church leaders were so burdened that they became willing to do whatever it took in prayer to save their country. Their late-night prayer meetings united them together as they exhorted God for change.

Nigel asks: What does 'exhortation' mean?

 When we feel like we're running out of steam, sometimes it's good to reflect on what God has already done and how great he is. We strongly urge God to move or act on our prayer based on what he has already done, and so encourage ourselves at the same time. Daniel's prayer in Daniel 9 is a good example of this.

Each location the church leaders met at was discovered, and they were forced time and time again to find a new place to pray. They became so desperate that some started to travel to the swamps and stand waist high in water nearly all night as they cried out to God to intervene in the destiny of their nation. There are stories told of soldiers shooting into the swamp in the dark, hearing the general direction of the pastors praying in the hope that they would hit them; fortunately they didn't.

The exhortations continued for months and months, until finally a man by the name of Yumeri Museveni pulled together an army and overthrew the dictator Idi Amin.

This all happened over twenty years ago. On my first trip to Uganda I can remember seeing streets that ten years or so before were filled with dead bodies. Now, the very things the pastors had prayed for have become reality. The country has experienced a huge turnaround, with the church exploding in revival and Jesus being openly spoken about on the streets. Just a few years ago, the president and his wife along with the same pastors that had been praying in disease-ridden swampland, held a meeting in the biggest football stadium in central Africa. They weren't interested in football but were meeting to celebrate what God had done. Packed out with 75,000 Christians, the president dedicated the nation back to the purposes of God for the next thousand years.

What caused this turnaround? The exhortations of these faithful church leaders. When speaking to some of them, they explained to me that shortly before Idi Amin was overthrown, they had a spiritual confidence that the dictator was on his way out. Their prayers became far more bold and they started to pray and declare the type of Uganda they were going to see – a Uganda that economically was thriving, a Uganda where AIDS would be in decline, a Uganda where people would openly speak of Jesus on the street and in restaurants. Their bold declarations became prophetic as in the months that followed they got exactly what they prayed for!

Nigel asks: What do you mean by a 'declaration'?

When we truly believe that what we are praying for will happen, we are making a bold declaration. Getting into a place where we refuse to back down – we are making bold statements of faith-filled prayer, reminding the devil that Jesus has already won the victory.

Mountain movers

'I tell you the truth, if anyone says to this mountain, 'Go, throw yourself into the sea,' and does not doubt in his heart but believes that what he says will happen, it will be done for him.' (Mk. 11:23)

Jesus' advice in Mark 11 was to speak to the mountain and to believe that what you have prayed will happen. We cannot begin to pray like this without a relationship with God. Yet, when the burden of God's heart is at the centre of what we are speaking and doing, our prayer life assumes a real and powerful spiritual dimension. We can begin to pray with boldness and make declarations over situations, but only if our hearts are right before God.

Jesus continues, 'And when you stand praying, if you hold anything against anyone, forgive him, so that your Father in heaven may forgive you your sins' (Mk. 11:25). If we hold anything against anyone it acts like a bottleneck, and the bad news is that this is something that we have got to deal with. God isn't going to try and smash down our unforgiving spirit so that we can become great prayer warriors; rather it is something we have to deal with. He knows that most of the time we never deal with the pain, but suppress it, decorate over it and at best learn to skirt around it. There may be so many instances in our lives where we've been scarred by friends, family or situations we're in, that our hearts have become hard. An intimate prayer life demands a vulnerable walk with God and with people.

In most churches we will see a wide range of people in leadership or support positions. In some churches these will be salaried, in others they may be volunteers. I'm talking about pastors, elders, deacons, administrative staff, youth leaders and so on. Their function is to prepare and equip Christians to share their faith and to serve the Kingdom of God. Their activity often mirrors the functions spoken in Ephesians:

> *He who descended is the very one who ascended higher than all the heavens, in order to fill the whole universe. It was he who gave some to be apostles, some to be prophets, some to be evangelists, and some to be pastors and teachers, to prepare God's people for works of service, so that the body of Christ may be built up until we all reach unity in the faith and in the knowledge of the Son of God and become mature, attaining to the whole measure of the fulness of Christ. (Eph. 4:10–13)*

Whatever our churches call them, we all have leaders who are there to prepare us to serve and to help us reach maturity in Christ. As you get more involved in the life of a local church you may take steps of faith and immerse yourself in a specific ministry of the church. Maybe you go out and feed the homeless, or you share your faith on the streets, or you go on an overseas mission trip. All the time the church is giving you leadership and guidance and support.

'The devil is not terribly frightened of our human efforts and credentials. But he knows his kingdom will be damaged when we begin to lift up our hearts to God.'

Jim Cymbala, Fresh Wind, Fresh Fire

When Adam and Eve sinned in the Garden of Eden, plans were already in place for Jesus to come to earth in the form of a man to re-establish the fundamental link between earth and heaven. From the beginning, the devil in the shape of the serpent tried to destroy the relationship between God and humankind. That has been his strategy ever since. In the Old Testament we are told that Satan forfeited his privileged position with God in Ezekiel 28, and was thrown out of heaven by God in Isaiah 14, but it is in the life of Jesus – the fulfilment of all Old Testament prophecy – that we see real victory over the powers of death, darkness and evil. We are able to make our bold proclamations and declarations in his name.

There is power in the name of Jesus

We have already seen that the declarations Jesus made often led to people putting their faith and trust in him. By demonstrating God's character through his actions and words, he exhorted people to understand the potential that they have through believing in him. Jesus was, and continues to be, the ultimate example of a person making bold and confident proclamations. In John's account of the crucifixion we read of perhaps the greatest declaration of Jesus, 'When he had received the drink, Jesus said, 'It is finished.' With that, he bowed his head and gave up his spirit' (Jn. 19:30).

Those words 'It is finished' signalled that Jesus' mission was complete; his victory over the devil was won. The apostle Paul helps us understand the enormity of the declaration that Jesus was making on the cross and the awesome impact it has on all who believe in him:

When you were dead in your sins and in the uncircumcision of your sinful nature, God made you alive with Christ. He forgave us all our sins, having cancelled the written code, with its regulations, that was against us and that stood opposed to us; he took it away, nailing it to the cross. And having disarmed the powers and authorities, he made a public spectacle of them, triumphing over them by the cross. (Col. 2:13–15)

The devil might make things difficult for you in work or school, in your friendships and relationships. Being a Christian is not an easy ride. Yet if you proclaim or declare in the name of Jesus you will be more than a conqueror:

> *Therefore God exalted him to the highest place and gave him the name that is above every name, that at the name of Jesus every knee should bow, in heaven and on earth and under the earth, and every tongue confess that Jesus Christ is Lord, to the glory of God the Father (Phil. 2:9–11).*

The disciples learnt that demons submitted to them in the name of Jesus, and throughout Acts we see time and time again bold declarations and proclamations made in the name of Jesus.

When we make a proclamation in our prayers we are speaking in faith and believing that what we are praying about will come to pass. As we were reminded in chapter 3, 'Faith is being sure of what we hope for and certain of what we do not see' (Heb. 11:1).

Bold declarations

There is immense power in Jesus' name. When we begin to pray with bold declarations and proclamations our prayers can be prophetic for our own lives and for the lives of others.

Nigel's Ignite ministry is a good example of people making bold and outrageous declarations about themselves. I'll let Nigel explain it himself:

The whole of Ignite is based around the Ignite Declaration. It's a six-part declaration that we have challenged young people to make before God. Simply put, it is a proclamation about passionate Christian living that is listed below:

> *I believe that God has a special purpose for my generation and me. I ask God to ignite in me a desire to discover this purpose.*

I commit to

Include Jesus in my moral life, my thoughts, words, actions and relationships.

Grow closer to Jesus through studying the Bible, praying and allowing the Holy Spirit to lead me each day.

Network with other Christians in my city, my country and throughout the world.

Involve myself in a local church and respect its leadership.

Take the message of Jesus into my school, college or place of work and the world by praying, living and witnessing so that everyone may have an opportunity to know Jesus.

Explore God's will for myself and my generation and seek to follow it.

We encourage young people and youth leaders to make this bold declaration of discipleship before God. Young people read through the declaration, decide to live their lives following these statements, and tell God that they are willing to do so. Sometimes we will get a whole room of young people to stand up and read out the declaration boldly before God as a powerful proclamation of their beliefs. Each young person signs their name on a laminated card with the declaration printed on it, which they can keep in their wallet or purse as a reminder. We then offer resources such as this book, our website, e-mails and events, to remind the young people that their declaration isn't just a momentary decision, but a fire for God that will last a lifetime and into eternity.

If you would like to commit to the Ignite declaration you can do so online at (http://www.igniteme.org)

'Every new victory which a soul gains is the effect
of a new prayer.'

John Wesley, A Plain Account of Christian Perfection

We're going to end this chapter by taking a quick step into
history. Those of us living in Wales recently remembered
the centennial anniversary of the 1904 Welsh Revival. One
of the key players in this revival was a man called Evan
Roberts. While in Bible School Evan Roberts had a friend
called Sydney Evans, who once asked Evan if he believed
100,000 souls could be saved in Wales. Without a second
thought Evan replied 'Yes'. In a letter to a friend he
declared, 'I have prayed and asked the Lord to close the
gates of hell over my nation for one year.' These are bold
prayers aren't they?

One of the most fascinating statements he made was
just days before the great spiritual awakening started. He
declared that:

*'There will be great change. . . in less than a fortnight. We
are going to have the greatest revival Wales has ever seen.
We must believe God at His word. His promises we have,
and why do we not believe Him? There will be wonderful
things here before the end of the week.'[6]*

Evan Roberts preached in a little chapel in a place called
Loughor only a day after he stated the above, and this
meeting was generally held to be when revival broke out.
The newspapers counted 100,000 souls saved in less than
one year; we now know it to be the greatest revival in the
history of Wales so far. The revival accomplished exactly
what the revivalists had prayed for, as their faith and bold
declarations changed a nation for God. Who knows what
could happen if we prayed as boldly for our nation today?

'Father, help me to be a person that believes what I pray as much as you do. Help me Lord to boldly declare your solutions to the problems that arise. Reveal to me and help me understand the full power of the name of Jesus when I pray. Amen'.

6 STANDING IN THE GAP FOR OTHERS

This is where the rubber hits the road. Now it's time to put some of what you've learnt into practice. In chapter 4 we looked at how Rees Howells prayed for a friend who had tuberculosis and really entered into a deep level of intercession. He prayed what was on God's heart for the situation and stood in the gap for his friend in prayer.

Nigel asks: What do you mean by 'standing in the gap'?

Standing in the gap for another person in prayer is one of the greatest gifts you could ever give to someone. When they have no faith to believe that God can answer their call, you become the bridge between that person and God in prayer.

Carrying your friends to Jesus

In the gospels we read of the famous occasion when friends of a paralysed man carry him to meet Jesus:

Some men came carrying a paralytic on a mat and tried to take him into the house to lay him before Jesus. When they could not find a way to do this because of the crowd, they went up on the roof and lowered him on his mat through the tiles into the middle of the crowd, right in front of Jesus.

When Jesus saw their faith, he said, 'Friend, your sins are forgiven.'

The Pharisees and the teachers of the law began thinking to themselves, 'Who is this fellow who speaks blasphemy? Who can forgive sins but God alone?'

Jesus knew what they were thinking and asked, 'Why are you thinking these things in your hearts? Which is easier: to say, 'Your sins are forgiven,' or to say, 'Get up and walk'? But that you may know that the Son of Man has authority on earth to forgive sins. . . .' He said to the paralysed man, 'I tell you, get up, take your mat and go home.' Immediately he stood up in front of them, took what he had been lying on and went home praising God. Everyone was amazed and gave praise to God. They were filled with awe and said, 'We have seen remarkable things today.' (Lk. 5:18–26)

Jesus responded to the faith of the paralysed man's friends. They believed that if they took this guy to Jesus, he would be healed. I'm sure that they would have been concerned for their friend for quite some time. They may well have been watching the slow deterioration of their friend's health, helpless to do anything except pray for him. Then news comes of a visit from the Messiah; their hopes are raised and quickly they begin to think of the practicalities of getting their friend to Jesus. At the venue there was chaos; people had heard the great reports and testimonies from those who had already seen Jesus – even the religious leaders had come out in force, no doubt to try to find ways of discrediting Jesus, this young upstart from Nazareth.

When the group of friends arrived, they couldn't get in: there were people packed all the way out onto the street. If you or I had faced this situation we might well have given up. We'd have headed home feeling we'd blown it. But this was a group prepared to stand in the gap for their friend, and this gave them a determination and a faith to get the job done – even if it meant making an entrance through the roof. Imagine the scene. Below, someone in the crowd looks up and spots the strange going on, as everyone hears this funny scraping sound as the tiles are slid one at a time from beneath each other. By now the crowd below and even Jesus himself must have been curious as to see what was happening. Soon the men tie ropes to the mat and their sick friend is slowly lowered down. The mat appears at the feet of Jesus.

Now realize here that Jesus is not immediately concerned about the man's health, but recognizes the faith of his friends: what was about to happen was not fuelled by the paralysed man's spiritual life, but by his friends' belief for a miracle. When Jesus says to the man that his sins are forgiven, he is in effect accepting him into the Kingdom and giving him eternal life. The man's physical condition is secondary to salvation, which is the greatest gift of all.

The Pharisees were outraged at Jesus. Who was he that could demonstrate such authority? Immediately the paralysed man jumps up from the mat, already saved and now miraculously healed. Imagine how incredible he must have felt, and imagine how excited his friends must have been. In his most difficult and desperate situation, his friends have literally carried him to Jesus.

When we hear of distress or heartache, sickness or pain, we might kick ourselves into prayer mode on behalf of those concerned, and that's great – it's the right thing to do. Some of those individuals concerned might not have any kind of relationship with God at all. So the fact that you are offering to pray can both impact their lives physically and spiritually. But what about praying for your non-Christian friends when there isn't a crisis? If we want to see as many people come to know Jesus as possible, we will need to be disciplined enough to pray that into reality.

Praying your friends into the Kingdom

When I was running a missions department in a church a few years back, we ran a 'prayer card' initiative where people could list the names of work colleagues, friends and relatives. The idea was that we all agreed to pray for those people until they came into God's Kingdom and recognized Jesus as their Saviour. Prayer evangelism was a priority for us. There were some people that didn't get hold of the idea, but others that excelled at it. Their faith ran high in belief that the people they cared for would be saved. It was as if the project gave them a fresh zeal and a new burden to pray at a depth they hadn't experienced for years. I remember one older couple reporting to the prayer group nearly every week that another person on their list had been saved. As they prayed, God was setting up situations for the people they prayed for to have an encounter with him.

Nigel asks: Tell us about 'prayer evangelism'.

Prayer evangelism is asking God to shape the circumstances of a person so that they have an encounter with him. In historical revivals such as the 1904 Welsh Revival there are instances where the preacher would pray from the pulpit for a non-believer by name; by the end of the meeting they sometimes arrived at the church and gave their lives to God.

Ignite run a similar project called ignition. It's a prayer evangelism idea, where you fill in the names of a few of the people you care for and commit to pray for them until they get saved. Then if they do make a decision you replace their name with the name of another non-believer. Remember that it's only God who can convert people, but your prayers do make a difference. If you would like a copy of the ignition card, e-mail us at info@igniteme.org for further details. I've often told people to tape the card on to the fridge, so that every time you go in the fridge, you spend a few seconds bringing one or more of the names on the card to the Lord, praying for their salvation.

I remember listening to the story of two friends of mine – Steve and Gill Houghton, who run a ministry called prayer week (http://www.prayerweek.com). They encourage churches to work together in unity and stand in the gap for their villages and towns. The ministry has exploded and 'prayer week', which is usually in May, is now running all over the world. Steve and Gill had two sons, Lee and Alex, who weren't Christians. They were both in their twenties and living away from home. Steve and Gill, like many Christian parents, had a burning desire to see their sons know Jesus. Within the space of two years, both boys made a commitment: one through stumbling across a website called (http://www.theshockofyourlife.com) and the other by turning up at a church, starting to attend and then becoming a Christian. Steve and Gill never pestered them, but arrested them in prayer.

I asked Gill how she prayed for the boys and this is what she told me:

I had a picture in the hallway of the boys, on the side table where we normally placed our keys when coming home. I used to get into a routine so that every time I walked past that picture I would lay a hand on it and pray for them. Sometimes the prayer was pleading to God for their salvation, other times it would be declaring the destiny of God over their lives. I spoke about the promise of salvation, not the problem of unbelief. It took a while to build up the faith, but I reached a point where I knew they were going to be saved. I continued this style of prayer and every time the devil would place thoughts of 'they will never be saved' or 'they are going to hell' I would boldly disagree and all the more state in prayer how wonderful it was that they would be saved.

Gill was fundamentally standing in the gap for her own children and took it upon herself to pray them into the Kingdom. At the time of writing Lee is in Bible College in Canada and Alex has been through a Christian mentoring programme in Florida.

'It is possible to move men, through God, by prayer alone.'

Hudson Taylor, God's Grace for Nine Generations

There's just one other testimony I want you to read before I go onto the last point in this chapter. I read it in a book by Wesley Duewel, called *Mighty Prevailing Prayer*. In it Wesley Duewel quotes a story he read by the president of Wheaton College who in turn heard it in person and had it verified:

About two and a half years ago I was in the hospital in Philadelphia. I was an engineer on the Pennsylvania Lines, and although I had a praying wife, I had all my life been a sinful man. At this time I was very ill. I became greatly wasted. I weighed less than one hundred pounds.

Finally the doctor who was attending me said to my wife that I was dead, but she said: 'No, he is not dead. He cannot be dead. I have prayed for him for twenty-seven years and God promised me that he would be saved. Do you think God would let him die now after I have prayed twenty-seven years. . .?' 'Well,' the doctor replied, 'I do not know anything about that, but I do know he is dead.' And the screen was drawn around the cot, which in the hospital separates between the living and the dead.

To satisfy my wife, other physicians were brought, one after another, until seven were about the cot, and each one of them as he came up and made examinations confirmed the testimony of all who had preceded. The seven doctors said that I was dead. Meanwhile my wife was kneeling by the side of my cot, insisting that I was not dead – that if I were dead God would bring me back, for he had promised her that I should be saved and I was not yet saved. By and by her knees began to pain her, kneeling on the hard hospital floor. She asked a nurse for a pillow and the nurse brought her a pillow upon which she kneeled.

One hour, two hours, three hours passed. The screen still stood by the cot, I was lying there still, apparently dead. Four hours, five hours, six hours, seven hours, thirteen hours passed, and all this while my wife was kneeling by the cot-side, and when people remonstrated and wished her to go away she said: 'No, he has to be saved. God will bring him back if he is dead. He is not dead. He cannot die until he is saved.'

At the end of thirteen hours I opened my eyes, and she said, 'What do you wish dear?' And I said: 'I wish to go home,' and she said: 'You shall go home.' But when she proposed it, the doctors raise their hands in horror. They said, 'Why it will kill him. It will be suicide.' She said: 'You have had your turn. You said he was dead already. I am going to take him home.'

I weigh now 246 pounds. I still run a fast train on the Pennsylvania Lines. I have been out to Minneapolis on a little vacation, telling people what Jesus can do, and I am glad to tell you what Jesus can do.'⁷

'Nothing tends more to cement the hearts of Christians than praying together. Never do they love one another so well as when they witness the outpouring of each other's hearts in prayer.'

Charles Finney, Revival Lecture VII, Meetings for Prayer

The prayer of agreement

Imagine being in a soccer match where you are the only player. You have to play defence, be out on the wing, up front as striker and in goal – all at the same time. Do you think you would ever win a match if the other side played with its full team? Prayer is a little bit like that sometimes, the feeling of the inability to go on, being overwhelmed by the task ahead and even a sense of giving up when things are getting too difficult.

In our football match of prayer you are completely exhausted at half-time; you've run ten times as far as the opposition, trying to cover all the positions and you've only touched the ball once. You were so glad when the referee blew the whistle, as you didn't know if you could go on. Then while drinking water to try and refresh yourself, one by one faith-filled prayer warriors join you on the pitch. They're in brand-new kit, well-rested and ready to join in. The score of 18-0 soon falls into the shadows. Within 10 minutes of starting the second half you have your breath back, you are playing with a fresh confidence. You're part of a team. The score is steadily climbing; by the close of play your team has won, by a score of 101 to 18. This is fantastic! You went on to the pitch feeling like you were going to get slaughtered and came off the pitch feeling like it was the best game of your life. This can be the difference between praying alone and with others.

Nigel asks: 'What is 'the prayer of agreement'?

The Bible says that when two or three gather in my name, I will be found amongst them (See Matthew 18:20). God likes us to pray together so we can agree with each other's prayer. A prayer of agreement is a little bit like an echo to God: a few seconds after one prayer is prayed, he hears another person asking for the same thing – prayers of agreement have much more impact than praying alone. We can also show that we agree with another person's prayer by saying 'Amen' at the end of their prayer.

The prayer of agreement does more than just provide an echo of what you prayed to God: the volume and weight of those prayers increases the measure of your faith. God thinks it's awesome that a group of people is so united in prayer that they meet to pray and intercede together for a specific thing. Prayer that is shared is prayer that is powerful with the presence of Jesus:

> *'Again, I tell you that if two of you on earth agree about anything you ask for, it will be done for you by my Father in heaven. For where two or three come together in my name, there am I with them' (Mt. 18:19–20).*

As we read in chapter 5, when Uganda was under siege from a dictator, the pastors united to pray and they agreed that they wanted their nation freed from oppression and to serve the purposes of God. In a smaller way, Nigel recently began to operate the prayer of agreement in his ministry:

> *In my regular travels as road pastor with Third Day, I am constantly seeking fresh ways to share the Bible with them. One of our most significant times together was when I*

chose to share with them the principles of outrageous prayer that Carl had introduced me to only a few weeks previously. The band and I began by studying the story of the paralysed man being brought to Jesus by his friends, and then we reminded each other about the prayer of agreement. We made a commitment to each other that over the next couple of weeks we would talk about the areas of our lives where we felt paralysed, where we had given up on an answer to prayer, where we were feeling defeated.

More than that, we would commit to pray as a group of friends for each other by turn, specifically praying for the areas that we were feeling defeated in. We were being the friends who took the paralysed man to Jesus and lowered him through the roof. In a way, we were praying the prayers for a person who wasn't able to pray for themselves. Gathering round an individual as friends and laying hands on them, we prayed for all sorts of things over a two-week period. Some of the outrageous prayers were for family situations, some for deeper relationships with God, others for personal needs that were as yet unfulfilled; one or two were for future band options.

Third Day had been together for over 10 years when we began to pray outrageously, and I had been travelling on and off with them a couple of times each year for 4 years. None of us had experienced before the depth of fellowship, honesty, and the powerful impact of prayer that we saw when we began to stand in the gap for each other.

So what would happen if you got all the Christians together in your school or college to pray for revival amongst the students? Or if you got all the youth together in your church to plead with the Lord for your city, town or village? What would happen if you stood in the gap with a pile of friends so that the drug problem in the place where you lived would reduce, or so that the crime rate in a rough area would be dealt with?

Can you imagine if this caught on and all over the planet there were people grappling with the major issues that face the places where they live? Can you imagine a time when the police realize prayer is so important that they ask the leaders of prayer meetings to advise them on how they could more effectively police the area, and feed information to the prayer groups for them to pray about? This is not a million miles away, we just need to start somewhere and leave the passion of faith-filled, standing-in-the-gap, united prayer speak for itself.

'There has never been a spiritual awakening in any country or locality that did not begin in united prayer.'

D.A.T. Pierson, www.retirementwithapurpose.com

Lord, help me understand the power of agreement, and let me find faith-filled friends who will pray for me and with whom I can pray for others and for impossible situations.

In the name of Jesus, Amen.

7 GIVING THE GLORY BACK TO GOD

'Prayer will open the door for God to do a glorious work in these last days. Prayer will stem the tide of evil.'

Chuck Smith, Effective Prayer Life

When all is said and done, prayer is a partnership or collaboration between you and God. It's not an activity designed to bring praise to the feet of any individual or group of people; the outcome of successful prayer will always promote God in the eyes of people and not pander to the ego of women or men.

Today there are more Christians than at any other time in history. The other day, Nigel was telling me that for every 1000 people alive on the planet, statisticians say that 329 of them are Christians. That's awesome, but that means there are 671 people per 1000 who don't yet know Jesus. The pursuit of the harvest is a relentless activity: it's an activity that doesn't sleep or take time off, it's an activity that cuts across time zones and language barriers; it's an activity that costs billions of dollars a year to facilitate. But then what is money if we can't take it beyond the grave?

Christianity is at its most widespread in all history and there is a lot to thank God for. Hollywood even made a film about the sacrifice of Jesus at a time when the church is busy re-inventing itself to be relevant in the twenty-first century. Most of the major language groups now have the word of God in print, allowing Bible translators to concentrate on the dialects within nations. With so much good news, we should be standing on tables shouting 'Hallelujah!' on the top of our voices.

'Prayer enlarges the heart until it is capable of containing God's gift of himself.'

Mother Teresa, www.gerrymkay.org/2motherteresa.html

Yet is it really so good? Or has the passion, desire and zeal for Christ which in the past has fuelled the church been challenged by a new form of attack – compromise? In my own view, compromise exists where the fear of God doesn't; where the respect and appreciation for the Lordship of Jesus is diminished in people's eyes. You could argue that people just don't understand what Jesus did for us, and that might be the case, but we are generally guilty of turning Jesus into a 'bless me' machine that we only call on when we need him to bail us out of the bad situation we're in.

Humility is the key

I often think about the many times when Paul in his travels writes letters to the various churches he has visited. Paul wasn't a brilliant writer and only actually wrote with his own handwriting once – but you can imagine him dictating a letter where he is caught up in greeting people and remembering the great times he had with them: the times they offered hospitality and the times where he recognizes the criticism someone has taken for the work he is doing amongst the new churches being established. Read these words from Paul to the church in Rome:

I commend to you our sister Phoebe, a servant of the church in Cenchrea. I ask you to receive her in the Lord in a way

*worthy of the saints and to give her any help she may need
from you, for she has been a great help to many people,
including me.*

*Greet Priscilla and Aquila, my fellow workers in Christ
Jesus. They risked their lives for me. Not only I but all the
churches of the Gentiles are grateful to them.*

Greet also the church that meets at their house.

*Greet my dear friend Epenetus, who was the first convert
to Christ in the province of Asia.*

*Greet Mary, who worked very hard for you. (Rom.
16:1–6)*

Paul, although very confident and accomplished,
constantly recognized that it was God who really deserved
any credit. In the passage above Paul is anxious to give
praise to the many people who have supported his
ministry, which is a recurring theme in his letters. He is
always thankful to God for the faithful lives of those
around him and he constantly remembers many individual
believers in his prayers. His sense of humility is such that at
one point he calls himself the 'worst of sinners' (1 Timothy
1:16) and is quick to point out that he owes his position as
an apostle purely to the grace of God. He writes to the
church in Corinth and urges them to pray with
thanksgiving for the mercy and grace that God has shown:

*He has delivered us from such a deadly peril, and he will
deliver us. On him we have set our hope that he will
continue to deliver us, as you help us by your prayers. Then
many will give thanks on our behalf for the gracious favour
granted us in answer to the prayers of many.
(2 Cor. 1:10–11)*

In every situation you may find yourself in, there is an
overriding need to acknowledge the great sacrifice Jesus has
made for you, and to give any glory back to God himself.

This is not always easy. I don't know about you, but my ego can sometimes be the size of a small country. I used to be very eager to speak in public so that there would be 'Carl' worshipping. I was becoming addicted to the praise of men: I loved it, and the more people who spoke positively about me the better. Then on one occasion in my quiet time I remember sensing that God was saying 'when are you going to worship me instead of trying to get people to worship you?'

I began to realize over the following weeks that my boots had got way too big and that I needed to start recognizing God for the awesome creator and Lord that he is: I needed to be spiritually renewed. How can we do this? One way is to tell God on a daily basis that you can't get through life without him. I have found the Psalms helpful for this – praying through verses and making them your own heartfelt prayer.[8] For example, how about Psalm 8 for starters? This will remind us of our place in the grand scheme of things.

O LORD, our Lord,
how majestic is your name in all the earth!

You have set your glory above the heavens.
From the lips of children and infants
you have ordained praise because of your enemies,
to silence the foe and the avenger.

When I consider your heavens,
the work of your fingers,
the moon and the stars,
which you have set in place,
what is man that you are mindful of him,
the son of man that you care for him?
You made him a little lower than the heavenly beings
and crowned him with glory and honour.

O LORD, our Lord,
how majestic is your name in all the earth! (Ps. 8:1–5, 9)

Nigel asks: What is 'renewal'?

 Remember the times when you felt really close to God. Renewal is getting back to that place from the spiritual dryness you have been feeling. It involves confession and a humbling before God.

Nigel asks: How is this different from 'revival'?

 Good question! The dictionary says revival means 'coming back to life.' It's usually used in the context of a whole church or group of people that is completely given over to God. When people live this way change happens on an incredible scale: communities, even nations are affected. God's presence is at the very centre of everything that's done.

Stories of revival

A sign of a mature Christian is that they don't talk about themselves as much as they talk about their Saviour. Their life is one given over to the purposes of God. In the great spiritual revival across Wales in 1904–5 a spark was ignited by a young lady called Florrie Evans. She stood up in her church in Newquay, West Wales, and said 'I love the Lord Jesus with all my heart.' Even though she had interrupted the preacher (which was not the done thing in those days – particularly if you were a female), her statement spoke of a deep appreciation for what God had done in her life. That church had been praying for some weeks for a spiritual renewal, but Florrie's statement spoke of something much deeper – a revival. Ironically she made this statement on 14 February, Valentine's Day. She spoke of the love she had for her Saviour on that day.

During the same year, God was working on the heart of a young miner, Evan Roberts, some miles away in a small estuary town called Loughor in South Wales. For several years, prior to the great revival that swept through Wales and beyond, prayer was a focal point in church. People were praying for God to visit them and I'm convinced in my own heart that this level of prayer activity made the lives of men like Evan Roberts a product of other people's prayer (see chapter 2). For two years Evan held meetings at Moriah Chapel in Loughor and travelled the nation speaking to groups of people in the open air. His message was passionate and didn't follow the normal preaching style of the day. Evan Roberts had four trademark points in his messages.

- *Confess your sin before God*
- *Move away from doubtful habits*
- *Obey the Holy Spirit immediately*
- *Confess Jesus constantly*

These four recommendations are great advice for us over a hundred years later. They certainly had a profound effect in early twentieth-century Wales. In towns and villages across the nation, hard men whose life consisted of going down the mines before the sun rose and returning from work when it was dark, were powerfully touched by God. Men who had previously wasted all their weekly wages by drinking all evening in pubs were now giving a full wage packet to their wives for food and clothing. The power of prayerful men and women arrested these men where they stood.

Evan Roberts was a man that wanted nothing else other than the glory of his revival meetings to be returned back to God. His heart was always thankful for his own salvation and the salvation of others. It was reported that several times in meetings Roberts would refuse to speak and simply lay down on the floor of the pulpit so people would focus on the presence of God rather than himself.

'History is silent about revivals that did not begin
with prayer.'

Edwin Orr, www.fob2005.com

Nigel has a great story about his involvement in the
centenary celebrations of the 1904 Welsh Revival:

*From the autumn of 2003 through to the end of 2004 I was
privileged to be chair of the steering group that organized a
series of events called '04theCity'. We were drawn from
church leaders and ministry heads from all over Cardiff
and our purpose was to use the centenary of the 1904 Welsh
Revival as an opportunity for outreach.*

*We took a big faith step and booked the Cardiff
International Arena for three nights of activities over the
centenary weekend in October 2004. In so many different
ways we felt underprepared, yet from the word go we
recognized that prayer was going to be central to all that we
believed God was calling us to do. Throughout that year we
could have succumbed to the pressures of a large budget,
with a potential shortfall of income; we could have
panicked about the slow sales of tickets for the weekend at
the arena. We were always trying to persuade other leaders
and their churches to catch our vision, and I was personally
aware that my own faith and relationship with God needed
to be constantly ignited if I was leading such an initiative.
More than once in our steering group meetings I confessed
that my feelings swayed between total confidence in God
and a total sense of inadequacy in myself.*

*One consistent theme during that time was prayer. I was
constantly praying, 'Lord, bring revival and start with me'
and the prayer of the steering group was always, 'revive us
Lord'. We had monthly city-wide prayer meetings when
Christians from across the city got together to pray, we
encouraged churches in their meetings to pray for the*

'04theCity' initiative and we made sure our own meetings were liberally sprinkled with prayer. We worked hard, but our dependence on God paid off. We came close to cancelling one of the evenings because we couldn't find an evangelist to speak, but then at fairly short notice Luis Palau accepted a personal invitation to come. Then only a few weeks before the weekend, our potential TV coverage fell through: with days to go UCB TV stepped in and did a fantastic job for us.

During the weekend at the CIA itself, over 9000 turned up, and our potential budget shortfall turned into a small profit. Most importantly of all, many people came to faith. I remember being overcome with emotion at the end of the youth evening; I had hosted the night that featured The Tribe, Y Friday, Rob Lacey and Luis Palau. Over 2700 young people had gathered together and about 300 came forward for counselling when Luis Palau gave the appeal. Our ministry team were overwhelmed and we only managed to get details of about half the youngsters who came forward. I collapsed into the arms of my wife with tears in my eyes, so thankful that God had been gracious to us. Over the rest of the weekend, our steering group met together to pray. We were pleased that our efforts had been rewarded, but we knew that actually God had moved, and all the glory belonged to him. We were so thankful for what God had done.

I once had the privilege of meeting an elderly lady called Nancy Francis. She used to live in sheltered accommodation and devoted the closing stages of her life to prayer for the persecuted church. Her income and outcome almost matched to the penny; she had no spare cash at all. Her desire to see the Kingdom of God expand was a lifestyle decision. She worked out that she could afford to send £10 per month to support a missionary in India if she only ate half the meal the local council provided for her.

Nancy would cut that meal in half and keep what was left for the day after. For years without complaint, and with joy on her face, she was thankful to God that she could make even that small contribution to the gospel at her age. What she didn't realize was the impact she had on people around her, including me. She was an inspiration and I thank God for allowing me to meet her.

The rod of testimony

We are going to end by looking at three Bible passages to help us carry on as outrageous Christians. In the very famous Psalm 23 David is tending sheep.

> *Even though I walk through the valley of the shadow of death,*
> *I will fear no evil, for you are with me;*
> *your rod and your staff, they comfort me. (Ps. 23:4)*

It was a custom in Hebrew culture for the father to present a 'rod of testimony' to the son and recommend that from the bottom of the rod all the way to the top, the child would carve out symbols to represent the times when the Lord had helped along the journey of life. Then during the difficult times, the owner of the rod could sit down and review what God had done, to bring encouragement into the situation, to raise faith and be spurred on. The reminder was that God had been faithful before and he would be faithful again. I'm not suggesting you rush down the local DIY store and purchase a broom handle and knife, but we can let the Lord ingrain those experiences on our heart and carry them around as a permanent reminder of his faithfulness. David managed this even though he felt like he was walking in death's valley.

In chapter 1 we saw how Moses had brought the people of Israel out of captivity and into the desert. The ultimate showdown was when Pharaoh wanted his slaves back and sent his army after them. Moses now had to face the challenge. With the army chasing from behind, and with mountains on one side and a desert on the other, the only way forward was the Red Sea:

> *Then the LORD said to Moses, 'Why are you crying out to me? Tell the Israelites to move on. Raise your staff and stretch out your hand over the sea to divide the water so that the Israelites can go through the sea on dry ground. I will harden the hearts of the Egyptians so that they will go in after them. And I will gain glory through Pharaoh and all his army, through his chariots and his horsemen. (Ex. 14:15–17)*

God's instructions were clear and without mistake. Moses was to hold up the rod of testimony and then reach out with the other arm and command the sea to part. Why did God bother to tell him to hold up the staff? Simply, he knew the fear in Moses' heart and he also knew Moses needed encouragement to stand out in this level of risk and faith. Inscribed on the staff would be all the memorable experiences of when God had been with Moses. He would have held that up: right in front of his own eyes there was the evidence that God was faithful. His fear subsided and his faith arose; his other arm was extended and with a thundering roar the waters began to part.

In the book of Hebrews we are told of Jacob's reliance on his staff:

> *By faith Jacob, when he was dying, blessed each of Joseph's sons, and worshipped as he leaned on the top of his staff. (Heb. 11:21)*

When his own energy was fading, Jacob was able to lean on his staff for support. His rod of testament had taken him from place to place and brought grief and separation to his family, but as he dies he is able to gather his sons together and worship God.

Now most of us would say that we aren't giants of the faith like Moses or Jacob or David. Yet we can learn from their reliance and trust in God. We could list many times when God has been faithful to us and when our prayers have been answered. We should be able to look at our imaginary 'rod of testimony' and heap glory on God for the great things he has done in our lives. Can you remember the times when God has helped you overcome a seemingly impossible situation? When God has comforted you when you have been fearful and close to despair? When you have been weak and close to collapse and only God has held you up? Each time this happens, the weighing scales of life are readjusted. Finally a day comes when you start to see the scales move as you firmly believe and accept what God is doing and has done. You start to get excited and look forward to the next answered prayer as you see those scales tipping you to the side of the Kingdom of God.

I know in my own walk that I have been so thankful to see God at work. I would not be able to deny what he has done, even if I wanted to. The times on mission trips when things were going horribly wrong and then within hours everything had turned around; the times of provision, the times of seeing people healed. These events have been breathtaking.

When the enemy comes with doubts and fears now, I compare them to what I know is true in my walk with God. When I'm praying for someone and the enemy says, 'Don't bother it will never work', I can say that God has been faithful before and he will continue to be faithful. Then when God does come through, with gladness in my heart I openly thank the Father for all he has done, and give the glory back to him.

The best way to live is to talk to God on a daily basis: thanking God for the sun that warms and the air that we breathe, praising him for his goodness and provision. You'll be fired up, knowing that when you pray for your friends they will be one prayer closer to salvation than yesterday, and because you are busy taking care of God's business, you have the comfort of knowing that God is busy taking care of you. Even when we have experienced the greatest victories in prayer we should remember it's all about God not about us. Our cry to God each day should be like this:

Yours, O LORD, is the greatness and the power
and the glory and the majesty and the splendour,
for everything in heaven and earth is yours.
Yours, O LORD, is the kingdom;
you are exalted as head over all. (1 Chr. 29:11)

'Avail yourself of the greatest privilege this side of heaven. Jesus Christ died to make this communion with the Father possible.'
Billy Graham, www.psalm121.ca/quotes/dcqgraham

Thank you God for the opportunity to share with people, in the writing of this book, for being able to encourage and teach and also for the journey you have brought us on. Today God we want to give you glory in all that we do. We give you glory for saving us, for allowing us to express ourselves, for the fact that we can worship you in freedom and truth. Jesus, you are awesome and we just want to serve you more each day. Amen.

Appendix:

PRAYER AND FASTING

Fasting means to voluntarily deprive yourself of food or other comforts for a time in order to give yourself more fully to prayer.

Why do people fast?

Fasting is a demonstration to God that we mean what we pray. It is an outward expression of the commitment that lies behind the prayer. Fasting was an important part of the prayer life of many biblical characters, and has since been practised by the Christian Church throughout its history. If we look in the Bible we see that there are different reasons for why people fasted:

- *To hear from God (Acts 13:2)*
- *To seek God's special help or blessing (2 Chr. 20: 1–4; Ezra 8:21–23)*
- *To express repentance (Neh. 9:1–2)*
- *To petition God to fulfil his word (Dan. 9:1–3)*
- *To turn aside God's Judgement (2 Chr. 7:13–14)*[9]

Guides and principles

There are some guidelines and principles that are worth mentioning before you start on a fast. We hope that you find these helpful.

You should never fast because. . .

• *Someone else is putting pressure on you to do so*
Your fasting must stem from your personal choice and be based on your own convictions. You must not fast because someone asks you to, because you don't want to look less committed than others or because you feel that it is expected of you.

• *Fasting will make others recognize the strength of your spiritual life*
Jesus said that you should not fast in order to be noticed by others. Rather, fasting is something between you and your heavenly father, who will reward you for what is done in secret (Mt. 6:18).

• *You want to punish yourself for a sinful life*
'[Jesus] himself bore our sins in his body on the tree' (1 Pet. 2:24). God forgives our sins, and doesn't want us to punish ourselves for them.

How to fast safely

If you are a healthy full-grown adult, fasting within the following guidelines should not normally cause any damage to your health. Nonetheless, we would encourage anyone wishing to fast to consult with their doctor first – especially if you are pregnant, on medication or suffering from illness of any kind. If you are not used to fasting, it is recommended that you start with a short fast (one to three days). If you don't experience any difficulties with this, then you can gradually increase the length of your fast if you wish to, until you become confident at fasting for a week, two weeks or longer. An alternative to fasting for long blocks of time is to fast for one day or more each week. But again we are not here to set guidelines on how long people should fast for. This is a personal decision. See also the section on partial fasting below.

A healthy fast

• *Most people find that the first day or two are by far the hardest*
This is because your body is used to a certain rhythm of eating and drinking. Hunger pangs are your body's normal way of telling you that it is time to eat. During this time it is normal to feel hungry, and for your stomach to rumble. You may also experience mild headaches. After this first day or two though, the body quickly adapts, and people usually find themselves feeling much better. You don't feel physically hungry, although you may still have the desire to eat, especially if you see or smell tasty food.

• *If you are planning to give up tea or coffee, do this several days before you stop eating*
This is because your body becomes mildly addicted to the caffeine contained in these drinks. Caffeine is a type of mild drug that can cause you to suffer withdrawal symptoms, depending on how much your body is used to. Headaches, mild shaking, feeling cold and vomiting are symptoms, some more common than others. The withdrawal symptoms usually last for one to three days. Many people continue drinking tea and coffee as normal.

• *You should not stop drinking liquids during your fast*
If anything you should increase your fluid intake. Drinking milk or fruit juice whilst fasting also helps to keep you healthy. Sugary drinks such as hot chocolate or sweetened milk give you extra energy and make it much easier to continue your daily routine. One salted drink per day is also recommended, as your muscles need salt to avoid getting cramps.

• *It is normal to have less physical strength and energy during a fast*
It is not recommended to fast if your work or daily routine is physically demanding. It is also not recommended to

play sport or take part in other strenuous activities during a fast.

• *It is normal to sleep less during a fast*
This is because your stomach uses a large amount of energy to digest your food. When your stomach is empty, therefore, this energy is available for the rest of the body to use. Many people find that during a fast, they have a much clearer mind, for the same reason.

• *It is also normal to feel much colder when fasting*
The activity of digesting your food provides your body with much of its heat. Make sure that you keep warm and wear extra clothes if necessary.

If you are planning to fast for more than a week ask a friend to keep a check on your health during the fast. We would recommend that you don't fast for more than 20 days unless you are in excellent health and are experienced at fasting. It is a good idea to take vitamin and mineral supplements during a fast of 3 days or more.

Finishing the fast

After several days of fasting your digestive system is at rest. It is important to break your fast gradually, to avoid possible problems with your digestion. If you have fasted on water only, it is wise to break your fast with soup, fruit juice or milk. You should also restart your intake of food gradually. Soup, fruit, bread, or vegetables cooked in water are good. It is wise to avoid too much meat and foods that contain a lot of fat or spices for the first few days. Make sure that you eat slowly and chew well. A fast that has been carefully monitored can be very beneficial for your health. In our Western society our bodies often suffer from the consequences of overeating.

Partial fasting

Partial fasting was also practised in the Bible. For example Daniel and his friends chose to eat only vegetables and water for a period of three years as a way of seeking God and setting themselves apart from the luxuries of the royal court of Babylon (Dan. 1:5–20). Later in the same book, we see Daniel taking part in a different type of partial fast for three weeks (Dan. 10:2–3).

Partial fasting today

If you want to fast, but are unable to do so for reasons of health or work, a partial fast could be the answer for you. Everyone should be able to find a partial fast that would suit their physical condition or lifestyle.

Today you could partially fast by:

• *Avoiding certain food*
Choose in advance what you will and will not eat, and for how long you will keep it up.

• *Eating less often*
For example, miss one meal each day, and use the extra time to pray.

• *Eat normally, but drink only water*

• *Fast some activity that you enjoy, for example television or sport*

This appendix has been adapted with permission from La France 2002, A Prayer Guide by John Beynon.[10]

IGNITION

Ignition is an initiative that is all about you
- *Taking responsibility for your generation*
- *Praying for your friends who aren't Christians*
- *Being creative in sharing Jesus with those friends*
- *Igniting the fire of good news all around us*

Ignition is part of the IGNITE discipleship declaration and is ideal for youth groups, Christian unions, groups of friends or individuals.

The strategy is simple.

Tell God about your friends:
- *Take an IGNITION prayer card and write down the name of three friends who aren't yet Christians*
- *Commit to pray for them*

Tell your friends about God:
- *Plan an ignition event where you will invite those friends to hear about Jesus*

Tell us what's been happening.
Let us know what you are planning and how you get on.

RESOURCES

The IGNITE discipleship declaration that is featured throughout this book is an initiative of the Cardiff-based ministry Big Ideas. At the last count over 3000 young people have signed it. You can do so online at {http://www.igniteme.org} for free, but if you would like the declaration on a laminated card as most young people do, then this will cost £2 including postage.

Ignition is a prayer and evangelism project aimed to challenge young people and youth groups to pray for their unconverted friends and to share the good news of Jesus with them.

Ignite internships offer young people the opportunity of a gap year as part of the everyday life of the Ignite ministry team.

The Ignite Leadership Academy is a training programme open to 16-22 year olds and offers a one-night-a-week course for 12 weeks, and involves a residential weekend together. It is designed to produce inspirational leaders for the local church.

Youth leader resources are available to churches and youth leaders who want to encourage young people in their locality to take seriously the challenge of living as a disciple of Jesus. Our website has specific pages purely for youth leaders.

For further information on all of the above please visit {http://www.igniteme.org} or contact

Ignite, PO Box 39, Dinas Powys, South Wales CF64 4ZX
Tel: 02920 512247 E-mail: info@igniteme.org

To contact Nigel or Carl directly you can e-mail
nigel@igniteme.org or carl@igniteme.org

References

1. Selwyn Hughes, *My Story* (Surrey: CWR, 2004), p. 4.

2. Charles Capps, *Releasing the Ability of God Through Prayer* (Tulsa: Harrison House Publishers, copyright 1978), p. 47.

3. Charles Capps, *Releasing the Ability of God Through Prayer*, p. 74.

4. Charles Capps, *Releasing the Ability of God Through Prayer*, p. 97.

5. Quoted with permission from an article in *Prayer Magazine* Autumn 2004, European Prophetic College (Sweden: Media Support Services).

6. Kevin Adams, *A Diary of Revival* (Surrey: CWR, 2004), p. 87. Quoted from *Evan Roberts: The Great Welsh Revivalist and His Work* (London: Marshall Bros., 1906, eighth edition 1923).

7. Wesley Duewel, *Mighty Prevailing Prayer* (Grand Rapids: Zondervan, 1990), pp. 161-2. Used by permission of Duewel Literature Trust, Inc., Greenwood, Indiana.

8. See chapter 4 on 'Praying the Scripture'.

9. Here 'humbling yourselves' implies fasting.

10. For further information on fasting or for a copy of the prayer guide, you can contact John Beynon by e-mail (lafrance2002@aol.com) or telephone (+44 01482 882867).